Democratic Transition and Consolidation in Romania

Dragoș Dragoman

Democratic Transition and Consolidation in Romania

Civic engagement and elites' behavior after 1989

PETER LANG

Bibliographic Information published by the Deutsche Nationalbibliothek
The Deutsche Nationalbibliothek lists this publication in the Deutsche
Nationalbibliografie; detailed bibliographic data is available online at
http://dnb.d-nb.de.

Library of Congress Cataloging-in-Publication Data
A CIP catalog record for this book has been applied for at the Library of Congress.

Dragoş Dragoman, "Lucian Blaga" University of Sibiu, Romania

ISBN 978-3-631-76859-4 (Print)
E-ISBN 978-3-631-78256-9 (E-PDF)
E-ISBN 978-3-631-78257-6 (EPUB)
E-ISBN 978-3-631-78258-3 (MOBI)
DOI 10.3726/b15323

© Peter Lang GmbH
Internationaler Verlag der Wissenschaften
Berlin 2019
All rights reserved.

Peter Lang – Berlin · Bern · Bruxelles · New York ·
Oxford · Warszawa · Wien

This publication has been peer reviewed.

www.peterlang.com

Contents

Introduction

The election of Klaus Werner Johannis as president of Romania in November 2014 marks the end of a long democratic transition. Twenty-five years ago, the communist regime ended in bloodshed, with protesters killed in the streets by the defenders of the dictatorship. The general elections held in December 2016 close another period, a period of twenty-five years of political competition and alternative succession in power in the general framework of the new Romanian constitution, adopted by national referendum in November 1991.

The two recent political events are a milestone in Romanian politics for several reasons. Electing for president a candidate with German background and Catholic faith in a country inhabited in very large shares by ethnic Romanians of Orthodox faith is a proof of ethnic tolerance in a region generally marked by ethnic tensions. Electing a left-wing party, in fact, re-electing its candidates following a brief interim technocratic cabinet (2015–2016) means engaging for the first time in the logic of (re)electing parties with a fresh support as political reward. Since the very first elections held in the framework of the constitutional settings, the economic voting largely meant punishing those in office by redrawing their electoral support. The five previous term elections ended with the opposition being confirmed in office and legitimated to change various previous policy decisions, and sometimes strategic policy decisions. The two recent electoral events highlight a new stage in Romanian democratization, which is the engagement in a consolidation phase, marked by Romania's accession to NATO in 2004 and to the European Union in 2007.

Although this accession took place at a different moment than for other former communist countries in Central and Eastern Europe, which have been NATO members from 2000 and EU members beginning with 2004, Romania's democratic trajectory is much similar to that of its fellow former communist states. Although one could label it as a laggard, Romania overpassed a triple transition (Kuzio 2001), more complicated than the double transition undertook by other countries in Central and Eastern Europe. Alongside marketization and democratization through fresh institutional design, Romania and other countries in the region had to solve ethnic tensions that complicated very much institutional design and political competition. Many countries, like many former Soviet republics and former Yugoslav states had an even more complicated transition, since defining nationhood, securing inherited borders and accommodating national minorities added to the previously stated challenges (Kuzio

2001). Those states had a different democratic trajectory, with no end in sight. They are still incomplete democracies, balancing between East and West, mixing elections with authoritarian characteristics and severe restrictions regarding civil and political rights. In other words, despite being a laggard when compared to countries from the "Visegrad group" in Central and Eastern Europe, Romania is neither Serbia, nor Moldova or Ukraine. Focusing on fulfilling the democratic standards necessary for the EU accession, Romania even become the leader in respect to minorities' rights (Ram 2009).

Unlike Hungary and Poland, for example, democratic consolidation seems to have grown stronger roots. Despite an episode of "post-accession hooliganism" due to political actions and projects of populists in power between 2008 and 2012, Romania had not witnessed a conservatory revolution like that which swept in Poland and Hungary (Bozóki 2016), where conservative politicians in search for political resources over-run the previous elite consensus regarding the rule of law and the constitutional stability, a long-lasting process known as state-building. In Romania, however, post-accession hooligans, namely populist politicians in power, spared no effort in consolidating the executive power, opening the door to political partisanship and abuse. They also looked for institutional design changes that would favor the concentration of power, despising courts of justice or denying the neutrality of such institutions as those regulating mass media. They also get engaged in corrupt activities, legislative and behavioral changes that undermined previously stable normative frameworks (Ganev 2013). But they have been challenged and successfully tamed by ordinary citizens, engaged in large shares in street protests. This sudden activation of a new type of political action, namely protest, marks a turning point in the participation style of ordinary people, who seem to burn stages and get engaged directly in new forms of political participation.

The perspective used in this volume is, therefore, a combined focus on both citizens and political elites. On one hand, what counts for democratic transition and consolidation are the values, beliefs and actions displayed by ordinary citizens. Their social capital, social and institutional trust, as well as their willingness to take part in voluntary associations, impact on their political engagement. Social capital is important for the way citizens imagine commitment, solidarity, tolerance and political moderation, finally for the way they imagine political community. Their support for democracy is essential and should not be conceived as taken for granted. In fact, not everybody wants that democratic transition ends in full democracy, since defining democracy also includes social costs and benefits. Unravelling the importance of social capital for the support for democracy is an essential aim of this volume. Since secondary organizations are labeled as schools of democracy (Putnam 1993), their impact on the support for democracy is to be counted when democracy is defined in a competitive rather than in an idealistic manner. This is to say that democracy is not imagined as the best form of government, as it is currently defined, but as one of many plausible alternatives. Among those alternatives, the dictatorship or the military rule, people have to choose having in mind their real functioning, which they are aware due to more or less recent personal and collective political experience.

On the other hand, political elites are engaged during the democratic transition in a decisive political competition. Especially during the first stages of transition, their action is essential in defining the general framework of the competition, the resources and the rules by which those resources are distributed. Despite their privileged position, political elites engaged in the early competition are not free from constraints. The first constraints come from the democratic framework itself, once it was firmly set in place. But there are additional external direct and indirect constraints, coming from marketization and from regional international organizations. Refraining from bending the general democratic rules would give to elites in power the legitimacy and the moral ascendance of attaining the political targets. For Romania, as well as for the other countries in Central and Eastern Europe, membership into the Council of Europe, NATO and the European Union worked as a powerful anesthetic, forcing political elites to restrain from selfish and undemocratic behavior.

The end of external conditionality is therefore an essential test for democratic consolidation. By comparing Romania with Poland and Hungary, for example, it turns that populists in Romania did not affect as much the state building process as Polish and Hungarian populists did. Due to serious contestation, they have been sanctioned at polls and had to abandon much of their political projects. It does not mean that their intention was not meant to transform the political system according to their own interest, in order to consolidate in power. It only means that ordinary people had to oppose through enduring street protests and to face the threat raised by police violent actions in order to constraint populists in power. Ordinary people found out that, except opposition parties, they had to face alone the coercive action of security forces, with no support from the main organizations from civil society. Although those prominent civic associations have been very active during the first stages of democratic transition, and have successfully managed to contain anti-democratic deviations of political elites, they decided not to oppose populists in power. Their ideological compatibility with right-wing policies put in place by populists, especially in social and economic domains, made them less active that one would have expected. The official condemnation of communism by populists in power worked as a powerful anesthetic for once critical right-wing intellectuals.

The decision of those right-wing intellectuals to refrain from publicly criticizing populists in power flags a deeper change in Romanian politics. Forcing ordinary citizens to face almost alone abusive political elites triggered an unprecedented growth of protest as a form of political action. Protest has thus replaced more conventional forms of political participation, making Romanian citizens to burn stages in their political development and to engage in the new era of cognitive mobilization. This is how the volume combines the two perspectives, focusing once again on the citizens' abilities to interact with political elites and to shape the political system. Quick mobilization through new communication facilities, in the era of new media, is a challenge for both elites in power and the political system. Democratic consolidation is now questioned by the capacity of ordinary people to discriminate when judging public policy issues and when controlling elected officials. Their incapacity of discrimination could lead to manipulation and abuse, to injustice, intolerance and violence. That is why a solid civil society is needed in order to balance the fast growing direct democracy tendencies. A strong network of vivid secondary organizations could provide the background for democratic ideas and responsible leaders, who could oppose to a future populist leader who would intend to take over a genuine unorganized citizen movement.

The configuration of the political space under the impact of new communication channels and facilities, and the reconfiguration of the public sphere by the communicative interaction of independent actors are the two research issues which can be derived from the combined perspective we assume here. This is a perspective putting together a distinct focus on ordinary citizens and one on political elites. Their interaction, as emphasized by this volume, already shaped the democratic trajectory of Romania and brought the political system beyond the incipient anti-democratic threats. Democratic consolidation, which is the new phase the Romanian political system has recently entered, is not exempt of threats and challenges. And the most important seems to be the growing trends in direct democracy, especially when it can be easily diverted by authoritarian leaders claiming to speak for the real people.

1 Regime change and transition trajectories

The democratic change that began in December 1989 was an open game, with various possible outcomes. Despite the euphoria that embraced citizens in the streets, and even despite the memory of those killed in the uprising against the totalitarian rule, democracy was not the only possible outcome. Looking back and taking a broader view, especially by comparing the Romanian case with the trajectories of other former communist countries, one can notice the extreme diversity of outcomes, ranging from complete democratization to hybrid, unstable regimes and even to completely undemocratic polities (Ekiert, Kubik and Vachudova 2007; Pop-Eleches 2015). From the vast list of favorable factors that could shape the political trajectories of transitional regimes, our approach emphasizes cultural factors, namely shared citizen values and behaviors. Generally grouped under the large umbrella of political culture, those factors seem to be crucial for democratic consolidation, while the first transformation stages, mostly institutional, have been completed. This chapter will review the main theories regarding democratic transition and consolidation, with a special emphasis on political culture as a set of required cultural elements that largely help democratic transformation.

Following decades of authoritarian rule, post-communist Romania faced after 1989 the difficult challenge of consolidating democracy as a space of freedom, dialogue and trust. Not only post-communist societies in the region needed robust democratic institutions, but they still needed cultural favorable conditions. Social capital and its consequences for the consolidation of democracy were somehow neglected by the early democratization literature. The early scholarly interest on post-communist transition mainly focused on democratization and marketization, since transition in post-communist countries was expected to follow the same pattern as it did in earlier South-American and South-European settings in the 1970s and 1980s (Przeworski 1991; Linz and Stepan 1996). These limited requirements soon proved elusive. It was then acknowledged that democracy needs more than favorable institutional arrangements, it desperately needs favorable cultural contexts. This essentially relates to a common space, to a public sphere that binds individual interests into common goals and commonly assumed values, norms and socially accepted behaviors.

The most obvious difficulty in building favorable cultural contexts in post-communist Europe was related to ethnic and religious issues. Following the 1989 revolutions, the region inherited national minorities, secessionist threats, and the subsequent need to define the basis for national integration, obtain legal recognition of inherited borders and establish a constitutional framework within a short period of time (Kuzio 2001). The failure to define such basis for national integration complicated furthermore the post-communist transition and, at first glance, divided the region in successful cases and laggards, which still struggle to build a common political space for their citizens (Ramet 2002; Ramet and Matic 2007; Ramet, Listhaug and Dulic 2011).

This division is less clear-cut as it might seem, since many countries in the region make continuous efforts to redefine citizenship and language rights in the context of democratization and Europeanization (Dragoman 2008; Järve 2003; Stiks 2010). Whereas citizenship relates to a rather neutral political community, language relates to an ethnically defined community, to a nation. The ongoing conflict between citizenship and language therefore challenges the use of minority languages, especially in ethnically heterogeneous regions, like Central and Eastern Europe (Brubaker 1992; Kymlicka and Grin 2003). Although the contradiction between citizenship and language rights is still a key issue of national politics and ethnic cooperation, Romania avoided the trajectory taken by Serbia in the context of Yugoslavia's disintegration. Despite a brief episode of open ethnic conflict between ethnic Romanians and ethnic Hungarians in March 1990, Romania partially solved the ethnic contradiction by reducing the tension between national-building and European integration (Dragoman 2012). Romania agrees today to abide by the European laws and practices regarding the use of minority and regional languages and has ratified the European Charter for Regional or Minority Languages. Although its implementation is only partial (Căluşer 2009) and sensitive ethnic issues are far for disappearing from the political agenda (Gallagher 2001), Europeanization proved to be a very effective tool in correcting EU candidate countries' political trajectories, especially with respect to human and minority rights (Pop-Eleches 2007; Schimmelfennig 2007; Tesser 2003). As we underline in the following chapters, this type of external conditionality had little effect on the behavior of the political elites after 2007, when Romania becomes a full member of the European Union. This is also noticeable for other countries, especially Poland and Hungary, which have been affected by the arbitrary use of the executive power and faced serious attacks towards liberal and neutral bodies, as courts of justice or other regulatory institutions, as those ruling mass media for example (Bugaric 2008).

1.1 The trajectory of political regimes in transition

The European conditionality may work in the latter stages of post-communist transition, as it was the case of Romania and as it is currently the case of

Croatia and Serbia, but in the early stages of transition, democratization itself is at stake. Comparing the political change with an exodus, only the departure is known. Following the breakdown of the communist rule, numerous trajectories and destinations were possible. They are today more easily noticeable, since transition seems to have ended in almost every country in the region with different results (Gel'man 2008; Møller and Skaaning 2010; Way and Levitsky 2007). Whereas some countries successfully managed to transform their economies and politics and to join the European Union, some other refused democratization and turned to authoritarian rule. The explanation is twofold. On the one hand, what accounts for the dramatic divergence among the erstwhile communist comrade states is the powerful and temporally resilient influence of overlapping social, economic and political legacies from the previous era (Pop-Eleches 2007). On the other hand, an actor-centric approach is also to be taken into account when analyzing the third wave of democratization (Huntington 1991), by focusing on the competition that occurred in the early stages of transition. The situation of unequal distribution of power produced the most stable and the quickest transitions, with the regime to emerge depending almost entirely on the ideological orientation of the most powerful (McFaul 2002). This means that in countries where democrats enjoyed a decisive power advantage, democracy emerged, while in countries where dictators maintained a decisive power advantage, on the contrary, dictatorship emerged. In between those extremes are to be found countries with equal distribution of power between the old regime and its challengers. According to McFaul (2002), the regimes that emerged are not the most successful, but rather unconsolidated, unstable, partial democracies. Those hybrid regimes combine democratic and non-democratic characteristics, in that formally democratic political institutions, such as multiparty elections, work to cover a profoundly authoritarian domination that abuses human rights and disrespects civil liberties (Ekman 2009). The diverging trajectories of countries in the region depict a very scattered image of former communist Europe, with numerous post-communist countries members of the European Union (including former Soviet and Yugoslav states) facing almost numerous cases of unstable democracy (Protsyk 2005a; Tudoroiu 2011), failed democratization, weak states and hybrid regimes (Protsyk 2012), and the return of heavy authoritarianism that is actually working in Russia, Belarus and Uzbekistan (Eke and Kuzio 2000; Ledyaev 2008; Spechler and Spechler 2009), not mentioning the disappointing aftermath of the 'color revolutions' that recently affected Ukraine and Georgia (Lane 2009). The perspective scholars have nowadays regarding the "colored revolutions" is much more diverse than it was shortly after the events. Despite their democratic promise, these events turned out to be not enough democratic and revolutionary in order to take them as serious breakthroughs. Although those "revolutions" (and especially the "Orange Revolution" in Kyiv in late 2004) represented a political earthquake and a serious threat for more authoritarian regimes as Putin's Russia (Horvath 2011), they provoked a mere public disappointment by a series of corruption scandals, judiciary mischiefs and the persistence of presidential clientele and of strong oligarchic groups that control the economy and the media (Lambroschini 2008; Ryabinska 2011).

The combination of the two perspectives summarized above, the *path-dependency theory* and the *competition theory*, acknowledges that transition is not at all determined at start and that number of factors could head transition countries towards any plausible outcome. In fact, transition can be so unpredictable in its early stages that 'democratization' should be replaced in the scholarly literature with 'regime transformation', since the final outcome of this transformation is not known and a number of citizens could not wish it to end in a full democracy (Mishler and Rose 2001a). The importance of citizens' democratic values is taken as an essential asset for successful democratization (Welzel 2007). Despite their previous experience forged in the political environment of the old regime, citizens may offer their support to the new democratic regime by continuously updating, modifying and balancing their initial beliefs through successive experiences during post-communism (Rose, Mishler and Haerpfer 1998). It is thus essential to understand how people evaluate democracy during transition and what is the level of their support for the new democratic regime, in a context marked by fragile civil society (Howard 2002a) and irresponsible and irresponsive political elites.

Democratization cannot be fully understood without paying attention to the special relationship between citizens and political elites in the new democratic settings. Citizens' influence, pressure and inputs are essential in controlling politicians in office, whereas political elites are responsible for the overall normative and institutional architecture, especially in the early stages of transition. Although the first chapter focuses mainly on citizens' values, norms, habits of cooperation and patterns of interaction, the pending element of democratization that are political elites is not to be underestimated. The second part of the volume is in fact dedicated to the way political elites in Romania shaped the general rules of the political game and distributed politically relevant resources during transition to democracy. Their responsibility is to be taken into account not only in the first stages of the democratic transition, when their interactions shape institutions and forge the formal rules of resource distribution, but in the final stages as well, when their group interest may collide with the general interest. The model of successful democratic regulation through checks and balances suppose the strong intervention of critical citizens, who manage to balance any attempt of political elites in monopolizing power. This is the cycle to be completed by the Romanian democracy, with a functional equilibrium of inputs and outputs that configure the political process.

1.2 Democratic transition and regime support

Attitudes against democracy are crucial, since democracy is a regime which desperately needs popular support for keep running (Rogowski 1974; Evans and Whitefield 1995; Mishler and Rose 1997). In many cases, undermining the democratic regimes was made possible by people's dissatisfaction with democracy in place (Dahl 1971). Moreover, during transition in Eastern Europe, incomplete democratic regimes may be for a longtime a mixture of democratic procedures and a clear lack of political liberties, combined with political elites' pervasive corruption and poor accountability. This unstable situation could even lead back to pure authoritarianism and the complete rejection of democracy (Eke and Kuzio 2000; McFaul 2002; Silitsky 2005; Blank 2008), as it was the case of Ukraine in 2014.

For assessing the prerequisites for full democratization in Eastern Europe it is essential to understand how people evaluate democracy during transition and what is the level of their support for the new democratic regime in a context marked by fragile civil society (Howard 2002b) and irresponsible and irresponsive political elites. It is the evaluation of democracy that is the most problematic in transition settings, since the evaluation should not be related to the ideal definition of democracy, as it is sometimes the case in various surveys where countries with different democratic experiences display very similar levels of support for democracy, taken as an ideal regime (Klingemann 1999). The evaluation should be made instead by comparing real regimes, by comparing democracy with its predecessor regimes as they were in a competition for citizens' support. While this evaluation is almost impossible in consolidated, long established democracies, this is still possible in post-communist countries, where the memory of the past regimes still lives today (Dawisha 2005). Moreover, the comparison between regimes and their relative performance is relevant for the definition people do actually give to democracy, since the definition of democracy may include not only values and procedures, rights and freedoms, but also economic and social rights (Hofferbert and Klingemann 1999), as emphasized in this chapter.

1.3 Comparing political regimes

Democratic transition and consolidation are not only political issues. Democracy is far more than simple institutional procedures that are supposed to regulate political action. Founded upon liberal values, democracy largely is a set of specific requirements that allow in the same time the participation of all citizens and their unrestricted opposition to those who hold political power (Dahl 1971). Based on specific values, democracy thus requires not only the instrumental support, but the affective support of most of the citizens. Yet this support is dependent, especially in the first stages of transition, upon the evaluation of the new regime. This evaluation is dependent, scholars stress, upon variables specific to human capital, especially education, economic influence, mainly income, and civic attitudes (Rose and Weller 2003). This is to say that evaluating democracy means not only to subjectively measure its performance, but to compare democracy with alternative regimes. Some authors even proposed a series of plausible alternatives to be compared with democracy, that is a strong leader, who doesn't bother with parliament and elections, a technocratic government or a military rule (Rose, Mishler and Haerpfer 1998). Not only they are plausible in the way they were already experienced by former socialist societies, but they are suitable alternatives to idealist measures of democracy, in a period marked by severe democratic uncertainty during the early stages of transition.

The alternative would simply mean to use the idealistic definition of democracy, by directly asking people about their satisfaction with the way democracy works. What would really mean their answers? How could citizens evaluate democracy in countries with essential democratic deficits? This is the paradox uncovered by Klingemann (1999). According to World Values Surveys, the only countries where satisfaction overpasses 50% of the electorate were Azerbaijan, Norway and South Africa, countries with very different democratic performances. Moreover, World Values Surveys recorded more satisfaction with democracy in Serbia than in the Unites States! The confusion persists when one compares the satisfaction with democracy in the two parts of the now unified Germany (Hofferbert and Klingemann 1999). Whereas many citizens from other former communist countries evaluate democracy by having in mind the occurring economic and social difficulties, German citizens from the former Eastern Germany benefited of unprecedented support for integrating the Western economic and political framework. Even so, the evaluation of democracy as a political ideal (as the best form of government) and as a functional regime setup by the common German constitution is different in the two parts of the country. The difference could be not only the result of different perceptions, but of different definitions of democracy as well, since citizens from the Eastern part tend more to include in the definition of democracy social and economic elements than their fellow citizens form the West, who stick more to procedural issues and values. In order to overcome such definitional trap, we emphasize in this chapter the competitive dimension of democracy, as a vivid regime competing with non-democratic regimes for citizens' support.

The different definitions of democracy may come from different expectations regarding the outcome of democratic transition in Central and Eastern Europe. When compared with the current transition period, the economic and social performance of the former socialist regime balances the severe lack in political and civic liberties. It is not surprising to unravel that the overall economic and social evaluation of the previous regime is positive everywhere in the former communist Europe. The social and economic performance relate not only to living standards and social benefits, but to the quality of the educational system and personal security. During post-communism, many people not only faced deprivation and poverty, but increasing threats related to inequality and corruption. Post-communism largely brought in massive social and more personal transformations that shocked Eastern Europe by the erosion and collapse of the social safety net, the sharp decline of living standards and the rise of permanent unemployment and poverty (Abbott 2007; Berend 2007). Additionally, most of the post-communist states experienced a marked increase in corruption and state capture (Iwasaki and Suzuki 2007) and a substantial growth in crimes generally, and organized crime more specifically (Holmes 2009).

This essential social change may affect the way democracy is estimated when compared to other political regimes, especially in the first stages of transition, when political issues and the general distrust in state institutions combine with the low economic performance of the democratic governments. Therefore, until full consolidation, meaning by that a regime that functions as a democracy by providing unrestricted participation and opposition, the new democratic regime is to be taken as 'incomplete' as it generally features a mixture of democratic procedures (the vote), accompanied by the consistent violation of citizen rights, rule of law and political accountability (Mishler and Rose 1996; 2001b). This unstable context is responsible for the final outcome of the democratic transition, meaning that political transformation could lead either to full consolidation, or to indefinite stagnation in a stage of incomplete democracy that combines partially free and fair elections with a large range of restrictions regarding effective opposition. The favorable support for democracy may not be sometimes enough, as underlined recently by Qi and Shin (2011). Although mass political attitudes count in the process of democratization, it does not lead directly to full democratization, since not all supporters of democracy take part in the democratic political process and demand that elites supply more democracy. In opposition to Misher and Rose (2001a), the authors emphasize that 'those who demand more democracy are 'critical democrats', who are committed to democracy-in-principle and respond critically to deficiencies revealed by democracy-in-practice' (Qi and Shin 2011, 246). These democrats, and not simply supporters of democracy, are most influential in promoting the process of democratization. No matter what definition of the support is given, it is obvious that democracy is not capable to work without citizens' commitment. This is especially obvious in cases where both citizens and political elites decide to disdain, undermine and finally get rid of democracy. Authoritarian regimes can easily overtake, sometimes with the full consent of large shares of citizens and elites, as it was the case of the 1966 coup in Argentina (Dahl 1971), where almost nobody had serious regrets for the fake democracy setup between 1955 and 1966. Therefore, very few protested against the military rule that suspended the constitution, abolished the political parties and elections and ruled by decree.

In post-communist settings, by balancing the two sides of democracy, as unveiled by Hofferbert and Klingemann (2001) in the case of the former German Democratic Republic, namely political and civil rights and economic and social rights, citizens form today a significant political body that critically evaluate past and future. It is not therefore a surprise to notice a clear decline in the 'realist' support for those new democratic regimes, especially in the post-Soviet countries (Allina-Pisano 2010; Ledyaev 2008; Sestanovich 2004). The downward trend of support for the new democratic regime is to be noticed not only in Russia and Ukraine, countries that had different post-communist trajectories in that Russia under Putin managed to avoid an 'Orange revolution' (Silitsky 2010), but in Moldova, Armenia and Georgia as well. In those countries, public support for the first post-Soviet regime declined quite dramatically and finally collapsed, with massive national electorates refusing to support the regime (Haerpfer 2008).

This low level of support does not mean that democracy, in its normative aspect, is totally rejected by post-communist citizens. Making a difference between the 'objects of political support' and the 'levels of support', Norris (1999) separates the 'democratic regime principles' and other objects and levels, such as 'regime performance', 'regime institutions' and 'political actors'. It is thus possible to identify those citizens who think that democracy is the best form of government. More than half of the citizens in the region support the normative concept of democracy. This apparent contradiction between the low 'realist' support for democracy and the high 'idealist' support for democracy can be useful in understanding the way post-communist citizens evaluate the former socialist regimes and the democratic prospects of their countries.

1.3.1 The support for democracy in post-communist Romania

The support for democracy varies in Eastern Europe in accordance with many historical, cultural, and social factors. As mentioned earlier in this chapter, transition was very much related to the previous state of fact, in that both institutions and citizens depended on their previous cultural and political experiences. In the same time, the success of democratization was related to the first post-communist experiences, including the social and economic traumas that often accompanied broader political change. Romania, for example, did not experience the dramatic decline in support for the post-communist regime as it was the case in many post-Soviet states. In the same time, the democratic transition was not without perils. As in other post-Soviet Eastern European counties, Romania witnessed a combination of factors undermining the democratic transition. The most important are the low trust in democratic institutions, partially due to poor institutional performance, and the disillusion of market transformation, which brought in massive economic insecurity, rising structural unemployment and poverty. The recent economic crisis reopened the debate regarding the political consequences of economic cycles, with the undemocratic far-right response to social and economic crisis in several European countries, and especially in Greece. The more recent balance between democracy and authoritarianism in Moldova and especially in Ukraine proves that democratic processes are not irreversible. In this respect, the democratic transition in Romania was as unpredictable in the 1990s as it was in other countries in the region. It is worth to remember that driven by economic despair, yet manipulated by political activists, coal miners from Jiu basin dismantled by brutal force the opposition parties in 1990 and even forced the first post-communist prime minister Petre Roman to resign in 1991, following the occupation of the parliament (Gallagher 2005; Gledhill 2005; Vasi 2004). This was the most serious threat to democratic elected institutions in the early 1990s. With the stabilization of the political system, the subsequent contestation took only legitimate forms, ranging from peaceful protests to casted ballots. In fact, a political learning process has taken place in the whole Central and Eastern Europe, with citizens and political parties' behavior being shaped by constraining institutions. Voting thus become the main political weapon, which was visible after only three rounds of national elections and reflected by the consolidation of the strategic voting and by significant declines in party system fragmentation, disproportionality and volatility (Dawisha and Deets 2006).

In this section, we will provide some measurements for the democratic regime support in Romania, while the next section will make the point about the democratic support in the region. We rely here on robust data taken from broader comparative inquiries, from either international surveys (as World Values Surveys) or from regionally focused inquiries or in-depth case-studies. The support for democracy is measured in all cases by using a realistic definition of the democratic regime (Mishler and Rose 2001b), as stressed above. According to Dahl (1971), the attachment to democracy is the attachment to a peculiar political regime that is largely imperfect, but fully perfectible, deeply tolerant and human. The liberties promoted by democratic regimes often loose charm, which is in fact their revolutionary charm. These liberties are more often taken for granted. But people who lost them or never had such liberties, are much more thankful for. People from Eastern European countries did not enjoy for a long period of time the benefits of these liberties, and by this they possess the historical experience enabling them to make a personal evaluation of political regimes. Those memories will plausibly fade as time goes by, yet they are still politically significant. As demonstrated for the German case, even two decades after the fall of the Berlin Wall, German citizens (and especially those from the Eastern landers) still have a good knowledge about the former regime and the daily living, making proof of a remarkable cultural memory (Stockemer and Elder 2015). One democratic indicator could therefore measure how strongly people reject some plausible undemocratic alternatives, and thus expressing the attachment for democracy as a competitive regime.

Quantitative analysis, as presented in Tabs 1.1 to 1.5, is one of the most reliable research strategies when it comes to study attitudes and values on a large scale and very useful when comparing countries. The democratic indicator built up in the case of Romania is done by adding the disagreement with the undemocratic

Tab. 1.1: Attitudes regarding the undemocratic alternatives in Romania. Source: World Values Survey, 2005.

How good would it be for Romania...	Very good	Good	Bad	Very bad	DK/ NA
To have a strong leader, who does not bother with Parliament and elections	28.9	36.8	12.9	5.4	16.0
That experts reach a decision, instead of government, as they consider to be the best decision for the country	22.6	37.6	14.9	3.8	21.1
To be ruled by a military regime	5.2	11.5	35.2	30.2	17.7

The figures in the table are expressed in percentage.

Tab. 1.2: Attitudes regarding the undemocratic alternatives in Bulgaria. Source: Center for the Study of Democracy, 2000.

	Strongly disagree	Somehow disagree	Somehow agree	Strongly agree
The president should, in fact, run the country	10.2	23.6	30.5	35.7
Experts should, in fact, run the country	5.6	17.1	36.7	40.6
It would be better if the country was run by the military	66.7	22.4	6.8	4.1

The figures in the table are expressed in percentage.

Tab. 1.3: The evaluation of democracy as ideal. Source: for Romania, Center for Urban and Regional Sociology, 2000. For Bulgaria, Center for the Study of Democracy, 2000.

Even it is not perfect, democracy is still the best form of government	Romania	Bulgaria
Strongly disagree	5.0	12.4
Disagree	16.4	23.9
Agree	41.1	36.0
Strongly agree	37.5	27.7

The figures in the table are expressed in percentage.

Tab. 1.4: Attitudes regarding the undemocratic alternatives in the Baltic states. Source: Ehin (2007).

	Estonia	Latvia	Lithuania
1996			
A strong leader should, in fact, run the country	39	45	62
It would be better if the country was run by the military	2	3	6
2004			
A strong leader should, in fact, run the country	25	30	27
It would be better if the country was run by the military	1	3	4

The figures in the table are expressed in percentage.

alternatives mentioned above. Statistically, the three items make up a consistent scale (measured by the reliability analysis Crombach's Alpha = 0.8106), meaning that the option for a strong leader is related to other undemocratic alternatives. Only 16.9% of the respondents do not reject any undemocratic alternative, making them seriously undemocratic citizens, whereas 48.2% reject one alternative, 25.4 % reject two alternatives and 9.4% reject all of them.

Tab. 1.5: Attitudes regarding the undemocratic alternatives in Moldova. Source: Institute for Public Policy Moldova, 2009.

	Yes	No
It would be better to have the Soviet Union and the socialist system back	40.0	32.2
You would vote in a referendum for Moldova to be again part of a new Soviet Union?	43.7	30.0

The figures in the table are expressed in percentage.

The political knowledge of plausible alternatives in Romania is built on the more or least recent past experience. On the one hand, the technocratic rule was frequently pointed out as a suitable option for new democratic parties' lack of experience and expertise in managing various economic and administrative issues. Romania was ruled by such expert governments in several occasions (1991–1992, 1999–2000, 2015–2016). On the other hand, the communist and the pre-communist regimes provided the experience of dictatorship under the form of 'sultanistic' communism (Linz and Stepan 1996) and of the military rule under the command of a marshal during World War II (Deletant 2006).

1.3.2 The support for democracy in other East European countries

The situation is not significantly different in other post-communist countries, despite some variations in the support for democracy. In Bulgaria, for instance, the support for undemocratic regimes is similar to the Romanian case. One should remember that Bulgaria was longtime associated with Romania in the process of European integration, in that both countries shared a common path in coming at term with the post-communist transition (Cameron 2003; Noutcheva and Bechev 2008). Both countries were invited to join the European Union in the second 'wave' of enlargement, at the European Council held in Helsinki in 1999, although the practice of 'wave enlargement' was later abandoned in favor of specific negotiations with individual countries, as it was the case of Croatia. The European Council held in Brussels in December 2004 decided that Romania and Bulgaria would sign the membership treaties at the same time in 2005 and be part of the Union in 2007, three years later then other eight former communist states (Hungary, Poland, the Czech Republic, Slovakia, Slovenia, Estonia, Latvia and Lithuania), who joined EU in 2004.

In Bulgaria, the non-democratic alternative of a personal, authoritarian rule is expressed by the exclusive rule of the president, who makes no appeal to an elected parliament or to political parties who form the government. In Bulgaria,

24.4% of the respondents reject all the alternatives, while 36.8% support one non-democratic alternative, 34.6% support two alternatives and 4.2% support all of them. Once again, the realistic measure of democracy in competition with plausible non-democratic alternatives makes a difference from the idealistic measure of democracy as the best form of government. The non-democratic alternatives are familiar to both Romania and Bulgaria, which experienced similar types of regimes. When asked about democracy as ideal, few people reject the idea that, in fact, democracy is the best form of government.

In the post-Soviet geographical area however, the current status of the former Soviet republics differs by and large. On the one hand, the three Baltic states (Lithuania, Latvia and Estonia) could be seen as a success story when it comes to set up both ethnic conflict management and European integration (Clemens 2010; Lühiste 2006). On the other hand, there is Moldova and other hybrid regimes (Protsyk 2005a; Tsyganov 2007; Tudoroiu 2011), and even Ukraine, which ended transition with an open military conflict with secessionist Eastern provinces, instead of a successful 'color revolution' against the previous undemocratic regime (Lambroschini 2008; Lane 2009). At the extreme, one can find Belarus, Kazakhstan and other former Soviet republics, which maintained for long time an authoritarian regime by making appeal to the former Soviet living standards and political style (Abbott 2007; Eke and Kuzio 2000; Gel'man 2008).

In the Baltic countries, the support for alternative, non-democratic regimes, is by no means different from that unraveled by surveys in Romania and Bulgaria. The surveys made in the 1990s and after 2000 display however a decline into the support for a strong leader, whereas the willingness to support a military regime was constantly low.

The overall situation is different in Moldova. As other hybrid regimes (McFaul 2002) that persisted after the dismantlement of the Soviet Union (in fact regimes that combine in various proportions minimal democratic requirements as term elections with serious non-democratic and even authoritarian features), Moldova is a weak state (Way 2003). It not only faces democratic challenges (Dragoman 2015a), but serious threats against its territorial integrity and inclusive citizenship (Dembinska and Danero Iglesias 2013), with a solid Russian speaking minority challenging the domination of the national language and the definition of Moldova as national state (Danero Iglesias 2015). With the persistence of Soviet nostalgia of good old days and with political parties that conceive closer ties with Russia as a fair alternative to European integration, it is not surprising that non-democratic alternatives have been praised during transition. The alternative here, which is hard to conceive in other East European countries, is turning back to the Soviet regime, in a way Russia and especially

Belarus have done (Blank 2008; Dawisha 2005; Tsyganov 2007). However, this is not to be taken as a clear willingness to reinstitute a Soviet-style regime, but rather as a strong nostalgia of citizens facing huge economic and social difficulties during transition (Berend 2007). The support for this non-democratic alternative is consistent. In a survey from 2009, almost half of the respondents (48.6%) acknowledged their regret for the breakdown of the Soviet Union. The downfall of the previous regime is seen as a negative issue by the majority of respondents, with a certain negative impact upon Moldova's current development (51.6%). The nostalgia may even turn into a real support for a Soviet-style regime, with large shares of Moldovan citizens 43.7% declaring being ready to vote for Moldova's integration into a future-revived Soviet Union. Once again, the question being hypothetical, the answers are to be taken with much caution. However, the partial success of Russia-Belarus-Kazakhstan custom union and the annexation of Crimea to the Russian Federation in 2015 prove that, even partially, Soviet nostalgia could live again.

The comparison of several cases demonstrates that the support for democracy and the rejection of non-democratic attitudes in Eastern Europe varies geographically. Whereas it is consistently high and stable among former communist countries that managed to become EU member states (Baltic countries, Romania and Bulgaria), numerous supporters of non-democratic alternatives are to be recorded in the former Soviet republics. The case of Moldova is therefore exemplifying for a hybrid regime that balances between Western conditionality and integration and the appealing Soviet nostalgia. The idealization of the past Soviet regime is in contrast to the current economic difficulties, the social deprivation and the political instability. The permanent shift between political forces in power, which look into geo-strategically different directions, may define an unstable and partially democratic regime, oscillating between past nostalgia and the promise of Western integration. This is clear proof that the trajectory of transitional regimes is unpredictable and that early democratic progress can be replaced by a solid backsliding. Finally, it is not necessary that transition ends with full democratization. Hybrid regimes may open into a full democracy, as they can turn into dictatorship or can survive into a long-lasting status-quo. They would thus combine democratic and non-democratic characteristics, meaning that some formally democratic institutions (as multiparty elections) could successfully cover an authoritarian regime, where human rights are abused and civil liberties disrespected (Ekman 2009). The prerequisites for the democratic support, namely the factors that would help citizens to support the new democratic regime during transition, will be discussed in the next chapter.

2 Social trust, citizen engagement and the role of civil society

When serious differences in the trajectories of post-communist regimes become visible, it was acknowledged that differences should lie in other essential aspects than formal democratic institutions. Although the pace of economic liberalization was different among former communist states, it was not the economy that fueled those different regime trajectories. Sooner or later, all the countries in the region had to move from the former centralist economies to more open and market friendly economic policies that accompany democratic institutional changes (Przeworski 1991). The scholarly research focused instead on other factors, namely cultural factors, taken as responsible for the varying trajectories. Those factors pertain to the willingness, knowledge and the abilities of citizens to get involved and to count in the political game. Their involvement is thought to be important for the way institutional actors, political parties and elected officials behave in shaping the political space. It is worth to underline here that the first actors in the transition process are much more important than the subsequent new comers, since at this early stage the actors in place have the power to set up the rules of the game, the relevant resources to be distributed and the legitimate actors who can be part of the game (Kitschelt 1995). From this perspective, individuals from the civil society, grouped in voluntary associations, could influence the complex democratization process by both defining the rules governing the distribution of power, influence, social status, and economic benefits and by keeping an eye on actors who should not be part of the new legitimate political process. This is especially true for former communist officials, taken as responsible for supporting and making previous totalitarian regimes work.

Post-communism in Romania is a period when, after decades of terror and exclusion, one largely notices the revival of democracy in terms of institutions, civil and political rights. Before 1989, people were forced to live in their own narrow private spaces (Völker and Flap 2001) and to let public space under the ideological control of the communist party. One would expect to see them after 1989 engage into public space and decide for themselves and for the community. People are free to participate but they seem to refuse to engage more seriously in public life. Yet weak political participation could be a marker of a deeper deficit. It might rather express, back in the early 1990s, the existence of an inchoate public sphere in Romania, a space of unarticulated interests and responsibilities. Romanians seem to largely disregard public space and to fiercely focus on their private life, by opposing their own private well-being to a negligible public no-man's-land. The rising individualism encouraged citizens to give up the public space soon after the dramatic change of power in 1989 and to not claim it back for many years. One plausible explanation why Romanians may neglect public sphere is because they don't feel to belong to such a place. Instead, they don't trust each other, cannot cooperate and feel powerless. With no perceived benefit, they eagerly accept to give it up to impersonal, obscure and distant forces.

2.1 Public space and civil society

Restructuring the public space is one of the greatest challenges of post-communism. Once dominated by the almighty state, which disabled citizens to really participate to its definition and organization, the public space seemed to be abandoned by citizens during early transition. The citizens' feeling of belonging to the public space is related to the common interest, which is the true foundation of the community. According to Habermas (1989), the public sphere (i.e., the public space) could be defined as the environment accepting the public political reasoning, an environment in which the individual can speak freely and where the arguments are not influenced by any political or social power. Thus, it makes possible for everyone to express himself regardless of any constraints on time, resources, participation or themes. It is the space created by the discursive interactions between private people willing to let arguments, not status nor authority of tradition, to be decisive (Johnson 2001). The public sphere was born in 18th century Western Europe and it emerged from the opposition between state and individuals forming the civil society. In fact, it had been created as an instrument to fight against the state, in order to guarantee a civil society that can autonomously organize and transform. It is therefore a political public sphere. Thus, public sphere is a medium for political justification, for putting the decision-makers to account, as well as for political initiative, and the mobilizing of political support. The public sphere not only enables autonomous opinion formation, but also empowers the citizens to influence the decision-makers (Eriksen 2005). Therefore, it is a precondition for democracy and self-government.

In fact, one might conceive two approaches in handling this essential modern concept of 'public sphere'. The first one considers the public space as the depository of the common interest, which should sufficiently motivate people to engage into collective action. The common interest should not be taken as a single, unified, ideologically determined interest, as the communist regime managed to impose it on the whole society. It rather should be taken as a common objective reality, which binds together the members of the community. According to

Peirce, objectivity and community are strongly related. 'The opinion which is fated to be ultimately agreed to by all who investigate, is what we mean by true, and the object represented in that opinion is real'. Thus, 'the very origin of the conception of reality shows that this conception essentially involves the notion of community' (Hartshorne and Weiss 1934).

The common interest may be tracked down as early as the Greek idea of polis, but the modern idea of common interest originates in the French Revolution ideals. Based on Rousseau's seminal writings, the Jacobins imposed their own conception of a society run by the state as the source of societal cohesion and the ultimate institution of the public sphere. Soon after the French régime of Terror ended, the public sphere underwent a structural transformation that favored the development of intermediary organizations between family solidarity and state bureaucracy, namely the non-governmental organizations merely focusing on assistance and support in providing human services (Wagner 2000). Two centuries after the French Revolution, stresses Wagner (2000, 547), the emerging paradigm of a decentralized and mixed economy of welfare, favored by the functional and structural transformation of the public sphere, serves as a strong corrective to the Jacobin assumption that the state is the only institution of the public sphere.

The second approach derives from this corrective assumption that a civil society, shaped by voluntary associations of citizens, works as an intermediate body between individuals and the state, by organizing citizens in a collective action aimed at limiting bureaucratic state power. This approach focuses on the political participation and on citizens' effort to influence the decision-makers. Democracy means more than elections, political party organizations and the protection of human rights, stresses Rose-Ackerman (2007). One cannot speak about a full democracy unless the policy-making process is accountable to citizens through transparent procedures that seek to incorporate public input. Thus, citizens and organized groups should be involved by taking part in the rule-making process with the government retaining the ultimate authority to issue general rules, but the democratic transition process in Eastern Europe has lagged in failing to provide transparent procedures that incorporate public input. Democracy means procedures that seek to incorporate public input, but it has to be clearly stated the will of public and organized groups to involve in public matters.

2.2 Social capital and the habits of cooperation

The pursuit of the common interest is expressed by the willingness to cooperate, on the one hand, and by the desire to refrain egoism, on the other hand. The two aspects are relevant for the political dimension of the public sphere. Social trust, reciprocity and altruism are ingredients for cooperation. And cooperation facilitates the development and growth of political resources of individuals, enabling them to form groups, to define common interest and consequently, to influence the political system. A society that achieves to set out interactional practices is able to create conditions for cooperation and engagement in the public sphere (Misztal 2001). Those cultural factors that encourage people to get involved into collective action with the purpose to count into the political process are embedded in the more recent theory of social capital.

These kinds of factors have been highly praised by the classic study of Almond and Verba (1963), but have been neglected since that time. The discussion on the importance of cultural factors in the democratic process was instigated by Putnam's (1993) research on democratic performance in the early 1990s. Social capital can be defined as a resource that helps individuals to acquire mutual benefits they wouldn't otherwise get, a social resource that makes people cooperate and pursue common objectives more effectively (Stolle 2000b). For Putnam (1993, 167), social capital "refers to features of social organization, such as trust, norms, and networks, that can improve the efficiency of society by facilitating coordinated actions." With such a loose definition, it is not surprising, emphasizes van Schaik (2002), that social capital appears as a multifaceted phenomenon which needs multiple indicators. This may explain why the measurement of social capital was made, according to Flap (1999), in an *ad hoc*, pragmatic and unsystematic manner. In fact, a growing sociological literature recently focused on social capital, that is the relationship between norms, habits of cooperation, and the engagement in the public sphere (Bourdieu 1980; Coleman 1988, 1990; Fukuyama 1995; Misztal 1996; Putnam 2000; Seligman 2000; Warren 1999; Whiteley 1999). Narayan and Cassidy (2001) have already made an inventory and have pointed out the large diversity of social capital measures. Although the exact relationship between the components of social capital remain unclear, van Schaik (2002) underlines that there seems to be an agreement on the main constituents of the social capital. At least two components figure in almost all definitions, i.e., *the generalized trust* and *the participation in civil society*.

Trust is considered important because it facilitates communication, the pursuit of common goals, and because it plays an essential role in solving problems raised by collective action. Fukuyama (1995, 26) defines trust as "the expectation that arises within a community of regular, honest and cooperative behavior, based on commonly shared norms, on the part of other members of that community. Those norms can be about deep value questions like the nature of God or justice, but they also encompass secular norms like professional standards and codes of behavior." Putnam (1993) turns trust into the basis of all cooperation between individuals. According to Yamagishi and Yamagishi (1994), trust is an expectation of others' benign behavior under circumstances where people do not have control over others, where they do not know each other. By contrast, assurance occurs in relationships where people do have control over others, for example where people know each other and are mutually committed. That difference might explain the levels of generalized trust and cooperativeness between different kinds of societies (Hayashi et al. 1999).

Social capital theory underlines that participation in voluntary associations, which is the second component of social capital, has direct and indirect effects. Following Tocqueville, Warren (1999) deeply believes in the importance of social capital for the good governance, that he disaggregates in three complementary domains to which the various associative venues of civil society might contribute: developmental effects on individuals (developing, forming, enhancing, and supporting capacities of individuals for self-governance); public sphere effects (constituting the social infrastructure of public spheres that provide information, develop agendas, test ideas, represent distinctions and provide voice); finally, institutional effects (supporting and enhancing institutions of democratic governance by providing political representation, enabling pressure and resistance, organizing collective actions, and serving as alternative venues for governance). Putnam (1993) also endows social capital with strong effects on democratic functioning. It would allow for greater control over politicians and for greater electoral responsibility, but also for a higher level of electoral and political participation. A responsive government, in turn, would stimulate public trust and improve democratic legitimacy. Following Tocqueville, Putnam (1993) has strong confidence in the ties between the habits of a society and its political practices. Civic associations, for example, would consolidate those *habits of the heart* essential for stable and efficient democratic institutions.

Participation in civil society could be formal and informal. It can refer to the engagement in informal networks or relations (that is being socially active) or to the engagement in formal networks or relations (that is being a member of a voluntary organization or/and doing voluntary work for an organization). Whereas the first type of engagement, the informal connection, is measured by the amount of time one spends with friends, with colleagues from work or outside the work place or with people at church, the second type of engagement is measured by the number of organizations one is an active member of. Moreover, another indicator of the formal engagement is the number of organizations one is doing voluntary work for. And, according to Putnam (1993, 173), it does not really matter what kind of organization it is about. The consequences of participation do really matter, while "networks of civic engagement […] represent intense horizontal interaction."

Ton van Schaik (2002) includes other two dimensions in the definition of social capital, namely institutional trust and the trustworthiness of the respondents themselves. Whereas the first dimension is measured by the particular trust in a series of institutions, ranging from the church to the press institutions and some international organizations as the European Union and the United Nations Organization, the second dimension is indeed more difficult to measure. The civic cooperation appears from the willingness to put groups or someone else's interest ahead of pure individual interest, from the disapproval of free riding. This disapproval of free-riding, emphasizes van Schaik (2002, 11), can be tapped from a battery of questions about the justification of behaviors like "claiming state benefits which you are not entitled to", "cheating on taxes if you have the chance" or "lying in your own interest."

There are however problems that operationalization and measurement actually raise. Should social capital be measured at a national aggregate, or at an individual level? Is it a personal quality or a relational asset? Putnam considers social capital as an individual quality, while other scholars take it as strictly connected to personal relationships, with no real social extension. For Coleman (1988, 1990), social capital is defined by its function. As with other forms of capital, social capital is productive, making it possible to reach some goals that would be impossible to reach otherwise. Like other forms of capital, social capital is inserted into the structure of personal relations; it is located neither within individuals, nor within the physical outcomes of production. Consequently, it cannot be explained by generalized trust. Seen as a relationship of commitment and reciprocity, it cannot be pulled out of a specific relation (a commercial one, e.g.) and generalized on a social scale. The social capital is generated by the relationship *between* individuals, rather than by individuals *themselves* (Rubenson 2000). According to Sandu (1999, 71), social capital is an aggregate of relevant values for sociability (a *productive sociability*) whose function is to reduce the costs of transactions and of social complexity. Again, its definition refers to a function, not to an entity.

It is obvious that social capital is defined in two ways. Coleman's definition is a structural one. Social capital is an aspect of the social structure; it is created by the participation of the individuals but it is not an attribute of individuals. Other authors, as Putnam (1993) and Newton (1999), define social capital as a subjective phenomenon composed of specific values and attitudes. We will use the second definition of the social capital in our inquiry about the support for democracy in Romania and in the region for two main reasons: 1. we believe that socialization may influence one's attitudes and values; 2. those values and attitudes may spill out from specific relationships and generalize at social level, in that people may transpose those values and attitudes – e.g., trust, honesty, commitment, and reciprocity – from a relationship to another.

The claimed link between the generalized trust and the density of a voluntary association network is another problem. Putnam (1993) does not clarify the relationship he examines between participation and trust. Thus, he does not make a difference between dependent and independent variables. After the beginning of the great debate over his alarmist warning concerning the declining social capital in the United States, Putnam (1995) excludes social trust from the definition of social capital and defines it certainly as a direct consequence of social capital itself.

Participation in voluntary associations generates a high level of social trust by spreading norms of commitment and cooperation out from the association itself. This can be called the *socialization hypothesis*. However, authors such as Newton (1999) doubt about this causality. The correlation between participation and trust generally found in numerous surveys could have been caused by a *selective recruitment* of the participants. The members of such associations are exactly those who have already displayed a higher amount of social trust, whereas individuals with lower amounts of trust do not participate. Thus, trust may be the resource that makes some people participate, while distrust would discourage participation among others. Though the socialization hypothesis seemed largely disproved, a new research has found a relative effect of participation. By testing the relationship between the two variables, Hooghe (2000) does not invalidate the selective recruitment hypothesis, but rather shows how associational life seems to produce some effects that are much better explained by the logic of socialization. Stolle (2000a, 2001) finds similar results and demonstrates how participation in voluntary associations works for the spread of civic attitudes and values.

2.3 Social capital and social benefits

These two difficulties, the measurement level and the sense of the relationship between participation and trust, influence the assumed connection between democratic values and institutional performance and social capital, acknowledging that trust links ordinary citizens to the institutions that are intended to represent them, thereby enhancing both the legitimacy and the effectiveness of democratic government (Mishler and Rose 2001b). Which of the two components influence democratic performance? For Putnam (1993), it is the participation. But if we dissociate the two components, as demonstrated by Norris (2000), social trust would be much stronger correlated to a series of economic development and democratic performance indicators. This is the only way the two components make together a variable that strongly relates to democratic performance indicators. Edwards and Foley (1998) conclude that we need to explore this relationship at an aggregate level, which is much more sensible to political and economic differences between different societies.

A number of studies have intended to prove the claimed link between social capital and the democratic performance. World Values Survey (WVS) turned out to be a suitable instrument for the numerous researchers. "The survey allows comparison of social capital in 47 nations, including a wide range of developing and industrialized societies, older and newer democracies, semi-democracies and nondemocratic political systems, and cultural regions of the world (…) The WVS allows us to compare measures of belonging to voluntary organizations and civic associations, and also provides a direct measure of personal trust that lies at the heart of social capital theory, and multiple standard indicators of political participation and civic engagement as the dependent variables," stresses Norris (2000). There are great differences in the level of social capital in the countries included in the survey. By combining the two components of social capital, namely civic activism and social trust, Norris discovers that Scandinavian countries, Switzerland, Austria, Germany and the United Stated are characterized by high levels of social capital, while Central and East European countries, Turkey and the former Soviet republics by low levels of social capital, with Latin American and far East countries at an intermediary level. Correlations between social capital and some socioeconomic indicators proved the link between cultural factors and socioeconomic development to be valid, even if they did not establish clear causality. The finding was that the link operates by the way of social trust and not that of civic network density. Although electoral participation and institutional trust do not seem related to social capital, the latter appears much more related, again through social trust, to civic engagement indicators, such as political interest and frequent political discussions. Finally, the tested link between democratic performance, measured by the Freedom House (FH) Index, and social capital proved valid. The dimension of the FH index most significantly related to social capital is that of civic liberties.

But social capital has many other benefits that support democratic values. The current section intends to offer an overview of the benefits of high levels of social capital. In the same time, several findings from various social contexts represent a warning regarding the threats that societies with low levels of social capital face. Low social trust might be related to inequality, corruption, prejudice and intolerance, fueling each other in a vicious circle that erodes the very basis of solidarity and collective action.

Engaging on the path of finding plausible social benefits for social capital, social scholars have examined various variables that seem to be related to social capital in shaping social ties and social values in a vast range of societies. In fact, trust seems to be related to some very desirable values: inherent values (as happiness and optimism for the future), but also political and economic values, such as a positive relationship between personal income and economic growth at national aggregate level (Rothstein and Uslaner 2005). According to Freitag (2003, 944):

> "Trust furthers norms, which abdicate egocentric calculations and self-interest. Moreover, it strengthens the willingness of individuals to act in the interests of the group or community to overcome social dilemmas (…) it stimulates a type of generalized reciprocity were altruistic behavior and obligations will be repaid at some unspecified time, at some unspecified location, by an unspecified person. Generalized attitudes of trust extend beyond the boundaries of face-to-face interaction and incorporate people who are not personally known. These attitudes go beyond the boundaries of kinship and friendship and the boundaries of acquaintance."

Consequently, cooperation may be undermined by any inherent lack of trust. Whereas trust could be seen as the basis of all solidarity, defined as the belief that all social groups share a common fate, and that is the responsibility of those having more resources to help those having fewer resources, trust may be weakened by sticky social characteristics, as social inequality.

Perennial and especially growing inequality erodes the basis of trust in post-communist societies. In turn, distrust may even influence the economic growth (Paldam and Svendsen 2001). There are strong findings to support this claim. Bădescu (2003) finds a quite strong relationship for 14 post-communist states between the growing income inequality, measured as the difference of Gini indices from the 1980s and from the 1990s, and social trust, as it was measured by the European Values Survey in 1999 and put forward by van Schaik (2002). Moreover, low levels of social trust are accompanied by the widespread belief that state institutions are largely incapable to fight corruption in these countries. Rose and Mishler (2001, 53) found a strong effect of corruption on social trust. As emphasized by the authors, "the more corrupt a country's current institutions are, the more citizens in those countries are likely to distrust other people". But corruption also affects trust in public institutions. Using the Transparency International Index of corruption, Rose and Mishler (2001) show how countries with higher aggregate corruption levels display the lowest levels of aggregate trust in institutions. Additionally, low levels of trust in public institutions may undermine a much required support for these very institutions, which are supposed to promote social policies in order to reduce inequality:

> "Persistent petty corruption may make *gift payments* appear to be rational responses to an unresponsive service sector: You may feel more secure in knowing that you can buy your children's way into a good school and to good grades, rather than risking more neutral assignment and grading criteria. You may well prefer to make an extra payment at a doctor's office rather than wait your turn. Corruption feeds upon economic inequality, low trust, and poor government performance. But it generates alternative ways of coping that may inhibit the adoption of programs that might alleviate inequality" (Rothstein and Uslaner 2005, 25).

Dysfunctional laws and state institutions, widespread corruption and impunity for many officeholders may nurture opinion that crimes remain largely unpunished and rules are systematically broken by those in power. They may also strengthen the belief that one can make a fortune only in such ways, by using perverted means, bribery and corruption. Therefore, solidarity could be seen as useless, because it appears contrary to the "winning strategy" in society.

> "Trust is closely related to corruption. The level of corruption is most likely to affect the level of 'positive' trust. If somebody commits an illegal act against you, e.g. ignoring the formal rules of a contract, then the offender will be punished in a police and court system without corruption. It is not possible for the offender to use the gains from the crime and split it with the police and the judge. So, if both parties know that it does not pay to break the rules, they will adapt their behavior and, by repeated encounters, build up trust and trust (...) When citizens cannot trust institutions in society and when everyone is not equal to the law, this unpredictability blocks the building of trust" (Svendsen 2003, 8).

Whereas democracy badly needs legitimacy in order to gain respect for rules, the lack of trust in state institutions and social distrust stimulate dishonest behavior in public life. Corruption undermines economic growth, affects state legitimacy, social trust and solidarity, in a continuous vicious cycle that is very hard to break:

> "We find that people who perceive increasing income inequality are less likely to approve of government performance and to trust other people and are more likely to support limits on incomes of the rich. More generally, when people see the government as corrupt and the country moving in the wrong direction, social solidarity (trust in other people) and confidence in the state will decline - and there will be increasing demands for curtailing market forces and placing limits on incomes. Most notably, people are largely inured to the petty corruption of everyday life; it is larger scale corruption - by business people and especially government officials - that threatens social solidarity and support for the state" (Uslaner and Bădescu 2005, 4).

The perennial inequality and distrust may generate a vicious cycle, what is known as a "social trap":

> "Poor and inegalitarian countries thus find themselves entrapped into continuing inequality, mistrust and *dysfunctional institutions*. High levels of inequality contribute to lower levels of trust, which lessen the political and societal support for the state to collect resources for launching and implementing universal welfare programs in an un-corrupted and non-discriminatory way. Unequal societies find themselves trapped in a continuous cycle of inequality, low trust in others and in government, policies that do little to reduce the gap between the rich and the poor *and create a sense of equal oppor-tunity*. Demands for radical redistribution, as we see in many of the transition countries, exacerbate social tensions rather than relieving them" (Rothstein and Uslaner 2005, 24).

A good example of the relationship between equality and trust comes from Sweden. Both political right and left criticize the encompassing social system for its supposed disastrous effect on natural solidarity in this wealthy Scandinavian country. According to Rothstein (2001), the argument put forward is that people stop caring when social problems and altruism are taken over by the government; compassion will be shown only through paying taxes and the informal social networks will be weakened. In fact, the welfare state would undermine natural forms of solidarity; it would undermine all intimate ties between citizens and, thus, would undermine even its own very moral basis. But there is hardly any empirical evidence to support such claims. Social capital has remained fairly stable over the last decades, and there is no evidence that the encompassing Swedish welfare state has undermined trust and social capital. One explana-tion seems to be in the way the welfare state system has been institutionalized, that is, the social policy based on the idea of "people's insurance" that supplies all citizens with basic resources. First of all, the universal nature of this insur-ance would prevent stigmatization of the poverty relief, so that people receiving support from the state social system cannot be seen as "the others", "the social parasites" or "the unworthy". Second, if one compares means-tested programs to universal programs, the latter are far less likely to create the suspicion that people are cheating the system (Rothstein 2001, 234).

Whereas trust is essential for the support for public policies, trust also strengthens the belief that other members in society do not cheat the system, thereby helping consolidate solidarity. In societies affected by mistrust and inequality, social groups view one another as enemies. The poor consider that those who made fortunes during the transition employed illegal means, espe-cially corruption, while the rich oppose supporting larger burdens favoring the poor, which they classify as "social parasites". This phenomenon is clearly re-vealed by redistribution claims in Romania, tapped by numerous surveys.

"(the) results suggest that people are aware of the high level of inequality and would like to live in a less stratified society, but with one important qualification: homogenization should affect mainly the richest people, and in the same time, the mechanisms for differentiation based on merit should be preserved or enhanced" (Bădescu 2004, 85).

In transition countries, inequality not only affects trust between fellow citizens and social solidarity, but inequality has effects on the way people accept social diversity and practice tolerance. It may be that social competition and lack of tolerance dispose people to trust their in-group and to distrust out-groups. Another relationship revealed at an aggregate level is that with social tolerance. Civic participation seems significantly related to the propensity to accept individuals with different lifestyles, social origins, or political values. This point is well illustrated by Sandu (2002) in his study of the European tolerance, which also uses World Values Surveys. The pattern discovered is similar to the previous: the greatest tolerance is specific to the Northern Protestant countries, Catholic countries are closer to the tolerance mean, whereas the greatest intolerance is to be found in the former communist countries. Once more, the social capital dimension most significantly related to social tolerance is trust.

With the evidence of the importance of social capital for equality, tolerance, cooperation, and economic growth, we turn back here to the political outcomes of social trust. While institutional design is one of the easiest steps during early transition, institutional proper functioning relates to the support institutions receive from ordinary citizens. Democracy, as a political system, needs the support of citizens, while citizens have to trust democratic state institutions in order to support them. The debate regarding the relationship between the two types of trust, namely between social (interpersonal) and political (institutional trust) is at the heart of the social capital theory. According to Putnam (1995a, 1995b), interpersonal trust helps make political institutions work because it "spills over," it "spills up" from individuals to institutions. But other scholars are skeptical about this relationship. The two dimensions not only weakly correlate, but they are theoretically different. Mishler and Rose (2001a, 55) found no evidence supporting the theory claiming that there is a close connection between social and political trust. From their evidence, interpersonal trust does not spill up to create institutional trust, and institutional trust does not trickle down. Interpersonal trust appears almost entirely exogenous to the political process. It is more an individual personality trait whose origins lie outside the scope of politics. By contrast, Mishler and Rose (2001a) stress that institutional trust is substantially affected by both political and economic performance, while being almost wholly unaffected by interpersonal trust or by socialization influences.

There are, however, findings supporting the claim that social trust and political trust are connected. Among the decisive determinants of generalized trust in Japan and Switzerland, for example, the strongest effect relates to the influence of institutional confidence (Freitag 2003). Newton (2001) initially stated that social and political trust tend to be expressed by different kinds of people for different reasons. Even if there is generally a positive association between social trust and political confidence, the relationship is not particularly tight or close, but rather weak and patchy. In subsequent studies however, by using more refined definitions of the two kinds of trust and more accurate survey measurements, he unraveled a stronger connection between personal trust, confidence in political institutions and satisfaction with democracy at individual level in twenty-four countries included in the European Social Survey (Zmerli and Newton 2008).

During post-communist transition, confidence in the democratic state institutions is important, especially when those institutions are under attack. Populism, from this perspective, strongly attacks representative institutions with the purpose of strengthening the executive power. This is true for other independent bodies, as the courts of justice and independent authorities regulating mass media, but core democratic institutions, and especially the parliament, have to be supported by committed citizens during early transition. This is not an easy task, noticing the bad relationship between citizens and the state that post-communism inherited from the previous regime, when the state largely abused power in order to tightly control society and individuals. This is even more complicated with distrustful citizens, who have difficulties in engaging in collective action and who feel powerless when it comes to face hostile and unfair institutions. It is thus important to estimate the importance of social capital for political engagement, on the one hand, and for the support for democracy, on the other. If it turns that social capital is important for the political engagement, but not for the democratic support, there is a chance that new political generations may engage into political action following the end of the democratic transition, while the merits of the previous generations are to have kept democracy alive despite all odds.

3 Social capital and the support for democracy in Romania

Social capital has been taken, as emphasized in the previous chapter, for an important asset for democracy. This chapter intends to determine if social trust and participation in voluntary associations really assist in supporting democratic values in Romania and whether those who participate differ from the general public in terms of political interest and political competence. If it be the case, those who participate are a hope for democracy, working for the dissemination of democratic values and significantly influencing the political system in Romania. Acknowledging that citizens from the former communist countries are not quite satisfied with the performance of their newly elected governments (Rose, Mishler and Haerpfer 1998), the weakness of civil society can threaten democratic consolidation in the context of internal economic and social crisis, when non-democratic alternatives could appear as radical solutions for harsh times.

As emphasized earlier, after the general breakdown of communism almost everywhere in Eastern Europe, democratic consolidation was seen in accordance with economic and institutional reforms. A few years later, the regional perspective was more shattered, with clear distinctions appearing in the performance of these countries (Rose 2001). Although the revival of communism is not a strong option, citizens from the former communist countries are not satisfied with the performance of their new elected governments and civil society is weaker than expected (Howard 2002a). Although the satisfaction with the evolution of democracy is similar to many EU countries, when the competing definition of democracy was introduced, nondemocratic alternatives were more strongly supported in Eastern Europe (Rose, Mishler and Haerpfer 1998). What we intend to stress here is the importance of civic activism and civic norms for democracy. We measure social capital by its two dimensions, *social trust* and *participation in secondary organizations*. Though institutional trust is not generally considered as a part of the social capital definition, it plays an important role in fostering attitudes regarding the democratic regime (Newton 2001). We stress the effects of these dimensions on positive attitudes concerning democracy, awareness of political system, political interest and orientations towards political inputs and outputs, with an emphasis on the support for non-democratic alternatives.

3.1 Social capital and democracy in Eastern Europe and Romania

When comparing social capital in Western and Eastern Europe, Bădescu, Sum and Uslaner (2004) found out that social capital levels in Eastern Europe were lower than those in Western Europe. The gap concerns in first place the associational membership. The proportion of people declaring that they belong to at least one association is lower in the former communist countries than in the Western European countries (4.7% vs. 11.8%). Another element to be considered is the time one spends every week or every month in organizations' activities. The time spent in those associations is lower in the former communist countries than in the Western European countries, as well. Therefore, expected higher levels of activism do not compensate the lower numbers of members in Eastern European associations. The gap in membership and activism is accompanied by a significant difference in social trust. The mean of social trust is only 2.6% in Eastern Europe, compared to 36% in the other countries, when measured by the European Values Survey wave in 1999 (Bădescu 2003a). This is the overall picture of social capital in Eastern Europe, where the young democracy benefits of lower civic resources that one would have expected when acknowledging the great enthusiasm produced by the fall of the communist regime back in 1989. The key question here is whether those limited resources in terms of civic engagement make a difference in supporting democracy as the only game in town, with the strong rejection of non-democratic alternatives or whether the democratic support rely on other political, social and cultural resources.

3.2 Measuring social capital and democracy in Romania

The analysis of social capital in Romania is based on a survey conducted in 2000 by the Center for Urban and Regional Sociology, at the Romanian Academic Society request, using a sample counting 1237 respondents, representative for the Romanian adult population. To accurately estimate the feelings towards democracy as a vivid political regime and to avoid measuring opinions about ideal democracy, Rose, Mishler and Haerpfer (1998) compared the support for democracy in competition with the support for other plausible alternatives. Even if the measure of democratic support may be questionable, at least this is a realist measure. We will measure the support for democracy on the same manner, by using data from the Romanian 2000 survey, as shown in Tabs. 3.1 to 3.5.

When asked about democracy as an ideal regime, Romanians proved to strongly appreciate democracy as the best form of government. When asked

Tab. 3.1: Democracy and non-democratic alternatives in Romania

	Even it is not perfect, democracy is still the best form of government
Strongly disagree	5.0
Disagree	16.4
Agree	41.1
Strongly agree	37.5
N	1118
	The president should – in fact – run the country
Strongly disagree	23.9
Disagree	33.1
Agree	25.6
Strongly agree	17.4
N	1075
	Experts should – in fact – run the country
Strongly disagree	4.4
Disagree	14.4
Agree	43.9
Strongly agree	37.3
N	1022
	It would be better if the country were run by the military
Strongly disagree	59.5
Disagree	24.9
Agree	9.6
Strongly agree	6.0
N	1050
	The number of nondemocratic alternatives
None	20.7
One	46.8
Two	26.6
Three	5.9
N	1237

Note: the figures in cells represent percentages. N is the total number of valid cases.

about competing nondemocratic alternatives, some important differences appear. The first alternative is the country being run in fact by the president, with no appeal to an elected parliament and to the political parties which form the government. Southern European and Latin American countries have largely experienced this kind of rule (Linz and Stepan 1996). Romania was also confronted

Tab. 3.2: Most people can be trusted

Strongly disagree	31.1
Disagree	32.4
Agree	32.4
Strongly agree	4.1
N	1217

Note: the figures in cells represent percentages. N is the total number of valid cases.

Tab. 3.3: Social trust and political trust in Romania

	Members	General Public	Urban Public	Highly Educated Public
Trust in other people				
Low	28.0	32.1	32.4	28.3
Medium	66.2	64.3	64.6	64.6
High	5.8	3.6	3.0	7.1
Trust in state institutions				
Low	31.9	33.7	35.9	32.3
Medium	63.5	63.0	61.3	63.8
High	4.5	3.3	2.8	3.9

Note: the figures in cells represent percentages.

with this governing style in the inter-war period. The second alternative is the country being run by experts, who make the best decisions for the well-being of the country, as they consider appropriate. This technocratic rule was frequently pointed out in former communist Europe as an option for political parties' lack of experience in economic and administrative management. Therefore, it is not very clear if this option actually reveals a nondemocratic attitude, or if it expresses an honest public desire for managerial competence, economic efficiency and nonpartisan involvement. Finally, the third alternative is the country being ruled by the military. This kind of rule, specific to some Latin American countries, is well known to East European countries as well. For example, a marshal ruled Romania during the World War II (Deletant 2006). However, the communist rule represented a political non-involvement for the military, in spite of its massive politicization. Therefore, the support for military rule is not so high even for those who display the greatest trust in the military. In fact, this is the least supported alternative in our survey. On the basis of the responses to the

Tab. 3.4: Impact of association membership on civic attitudes

	Members	General Public	Urban Public	Highly Educated Public
Impact of political events				
Low	19.4	17.6	16.7	15.2
Medium	51.7	51.8	49.1	53.6
High	28.8	30.6	34.2	31.2
Influence on political events				
Low	38.5	45.0	42.6	31.7
Medium	48.1	45.3	46.5	57.9
High	13.4	9.7	10.9	10.3
Political interest				
Little	21.2	34.1	26.4	19.7
Some	41.4	45.6	45.2	38.6
Important	29.1	16.2	22.6	32.3
Great	8.2	4.1	5.7	9.4
Electoral participation				
Yes	93.2	91.2	92.4	100
No	6.8	8.8	7.6	0
Party membership				
Yes	29.6	0	5.2	13.4
No	70.4	100	94.8	86.6

Note: the figures in cells represent percentages.

Tab. 3.5: Social trust, membership and political attitudes and beliefs

Variables	Social trust
Indicator of democratic attitudes	.063*
Institutional trust	.336***
Trust in state's institutions	.142***
	Membership in associations
Social trust	-.040
Trust in state's institutions	.024
Indicator of democratic attitudes	.104***
Political interest	.185***
Belief in the political responsiveness	.094***

Note: * = p < .05; ** = p < .01; *** = p < .001.

questions about non-democratic alternatives and about democracy as the best form of government, we compute an indicator of democratic attitudes by adding the specified variables. We use the indicator when discussing the relationship between components of social capital and democracy and therefore we call this a *democratic indicator*.

Since social capital theories are rather abstract, their translation into operational measures requires subjective interpretation. As mentioned above, for the current research, we will stick to the operationalization made by Inglehart (1997), which was reproduced by the World Values Survey. Inglehart (1997) operationalized social capital into two dimensions, namely trust and membership in associations. We measure trust by using the question: "(do you think that) most people can be trusted"?

One can notice from other studies how citizens of Eastern European countries display less social trust than citizens of West European countries generally do. By using the 1990 and 1995 waves of the World Values Survey and the 1999 wave of the European Values Survey, Bădescu (2003a) discovered that the mean proportion of trustworthy persons is higher in the consolidated West European democracies than in the former communist countries. How to explain this difference? We should not avoid paying attention to the question itself, because the answer largely depends on what *people* means. Therefore, a better operationalization of trust may be that of ethnic trust (Bădescu 2003b). Uslaner and Conley (2003) discovered different effects of generalized and particularized trust in the case of the American communities. But significant differences may be real. One explanation may be the socialization in dissimilar political regimes. The free expression of opinions is a different risk that people from these regimes assume. Totalitarian repression makes citizens much more cautious in establishing relations and less willing to freely communicate, features clearly tested by Almond and Verba (1963) in Italy and West Germany some fifteen years after the collapse of fascism. By using the 1999 wave of the European Values Survey, Bădescu (2003a, 124) also discovered a significant and positive correlation between the level of generalized trust and an indicator of democratic attitudes measured at individual level. The relationship continues to be valid when measured at national aggregate level as well, with no distinction for the geopolitical context. Therefore, the findings allow Bădescu (2003a) to conclude that generalized trust is a necessary resource for the quality of the democracy, with no suggestion for the direction of the causal influence.

In our research, we look at the relationship between democratic attitudes and several types of trust, i.e., social trust, institutional trust and political trust. The social trust seems somehow related to the democratic indicator that we computed. The correlation is positive, even it is very weak (Pearson R = .063, p < .05). Social trust also appears strongly related to institutional trust (Pearson R = .336, p < .001). The expressed trust in democratic state institutions proves to be significantly related to the democratic indicator, although it is rather weak (Pearson R = .142, p < .001).

As mentioned before, participation in secondary organizations is the second element of the social capital. Membership in associations is much less developed in Eastern Europe than in Western Europe. Membership in one or several associations (religious, professional, human rights protection, environment protection, labor unions, charity or sports associations) differ from the Western cases. Over three-quarters of Romanians are not members of any of these associations. East European societies have already experienced, during communist times, some effects of networks of informal cooperation, as Rose (1998) demonstrates with the Russian case.

"When a formal organization does not deliver and an individual cannot substitute the market or an informal network, three different types of network can be invoked to 'de-bureaucratize' dealings with an organization, that is, to find a way to make it produce goods and services. A person can try to personalize his or her relationship, begging or cajoling officials to provide what is wanted (...) The concept of 'blat' usually refers to using connections to misallocate benefits, as they are invoked to get an official to 'bend' or break rules (...) Connections, that is, asking for favors on the basis of being part of a 'circle' or network."

These are pre-modern tactics of getting what modern states provide through free market and efficient bureaucracy. But they prove that these societies experienced somewhat a specific type of cooperation. The main problems now, as voluntary associations become effective again, are different: the level and the type of participation, as unraveled by a study on Romania and Moldova (Bădescu, Sum and Uslaner 2004). The first observation is that both countries fit into a regional framework. Membership in Eastern European countries is lower, and when citizens are members in associations, they are less active. "(They) tend to have fewer resources and incentives to create new organizations or become active in existing ones. At the same time, the capacity of the civil society organizations to promote activism and provide incentives for membership is very low" (Bădescu, Sum and Uslaner 2004, 324).

The relatively low number of associations and unequal territorial distribution seriously reduces mobilization. Membership in associations seems to be influenced by social structure, and also by the attitudes people display regarding civic associations. Romanians spend less time with friends and consider friends less important than their Western counterparts. Their trust in civic associations is constantly low, as it is demonstrated by other public opinion surveys, as the series of Public Opinion Barometers financed by the Open Society Foundation in Romania. Voluntary associations must rely on external financial resources and on *a priori* settled objectives, which sometimes neglect local needs. In fact, Bădescu, Sum and Uslaner (2004) indicate that their members turn sometimes into private functionaries rather than into true civic volunteers.

The social capital theory emphasizes the benefic effects that membership in associations has on civic attitudes. Civic attitudes, however, do not equal our democratic indicator. While the latter indicates support for the current democratic regime and the rejection of non-democratic alternatives, the former reflect more an expression of the people's orientation toward the political system (Almond and Verba 1963). The civic attitudes include a vast range of citizen attitudes, as the powerless feeling (people like me can do little or nothing to influence political events), parochial attitudes (political events have little or no impact on my life), membership in political organizations, political interest (how often do you read political events in the newspapers, watch political news on television or discuss politics with family and/or friends). Although we are interested in how social capital impacts on civic attitudes, we keep on focusing on our democratic indicator.

Tested in several occasions, membership in voluntary associations seems to have certain effects on social trust (Wollebaek and Selle 2002). Social trust could be related to institutional trust. Therefore, we test the relationships occurring in our Romanian sample through a comparison of citizens engaged in voluntary associations, the general public, the urban public, and highly educated public.

Membership in voluntary associations seems to have a generally low influence on social and institutional trust. Those who participate don't seem much more trusting than the urban and highly educated public. The correlation between membership and trust in Romania is weak (R = - .040) and statistically not significant. The Pearson correlation indicator is negative, but its low value does not allow us to conclude about the impact of voluntary participation on social trust. Institutional trust, on the other hand, is not significantly related to social trust or to participation.

3.3 Impact of social capital on the support for democracy

Membership in voluntary associations would encourage those aptitudes that make individuals develop and turn into active citizens, making them surpass their subjective or parochial roles. Following the main thesis of the socialization theory, and especially that put forward by Putnam (1993), one would expect that those who participate in voluntary organizations to reject less the political output and to be more oriented towards the political input and the political system, as a whole. Therefore, we expect them to display a greater subjective civic competence, due to their awareness of the possibility that they have to influence political decisions. Hooghe (2003) demonstrates for the Belgian case that membership reduces the political powerless feelings. We also expect members in associations to be the most interested in both passive (voting) and active (party membership) forms of political participation.

Some effects of membership in voluntary associations are present here, although the differences between participants, the urban public and the highly educated public are not so impressive. The awareness of the political process, an indicator defining the civic culture, can be measured by the way of several items, such as the tendency to read political news in the newspapers, to discuss politics with friends and family, to watch political news on TV, or to listen to political news on the radio. We build an index variable for the interest in the political system based on the previously named indicators. In fact, membership in associations seems significantly related to this index of political interest ($R = .185$, $p < .001$).

The inquiry made by Bădescu, Sum and Uslaner (2004) led to similar results. In the case of Western societies, members in associations tend to display attributes that are more often generally associated with the ideal type of democratic citizen. In the case of Romania and Moldova, the countries under scrutiny in their study, the most active volunteers are exactly the most trusting people. They are more likely to support the rights of minorities and of unpopular groups. In both countries, activists are generally speaking more active politically. As stressed by Bădescu, Sum and Uslaner (2004, 337), "they have a greater sense of their own political competence, although they do not necessarily see politicians as any more responsive. Being highly active in an organization is not generally the key to greater political participation and a sense of efficacy. Instead, it is taking part in decision making that matters the most (…) Activists participate more and have greater interest, *but the key to believing that you can make a difference is not just taking part, but getting involved in the nuts and bolts of your organization."*

Bădescu, Sum and Uslaner (2004) have discovered an important difference between activists involved in the decision-making process and other members of the examined organizations. There is also a difference between members and the general public. The main problem is the quality and duration of participation. For example, in the case of the city of Cluj, where the field research was done, participation is no longer than a couple of years. Those who get involved in a later stage largely imitate the previously active members, but they stay no longer than their predecessors did. The risk is that they resemble more and more to the general public, which displays lower civic values. As Bădescu, Sum and Uslaner (2004, 338) emphasize, (ordinary) "people do not trust each other. They are not tolerant of minorities and other unpopular groups. They have fewer social interactions with friends and neighbors, and they join fewer voluntary organizations, do not trust their leaders, do not feel efficacious, and do not participate much in politics." In short, activists are the most tolerant and they display the greatest social trust. They could become opinion leaders and work for the spread of democratic values but, once again, they are few in numbers and their participation is too short in order to have some serious effect on the overall society level.

In the case of our Romanian sample, those who are members in associations more strongly estimate that politicians in power and in opposition manage to respond to public requests than those who do not participate (R = .094, p < .001), but correlation is far too weak. Membership is also significantly related to the measured support for democracy. Members in associations are not only much better oriented towards the political system, towards the *input* and *output* processes, but they more frequently display democratic attitudes. The correlation between membership and the democratic indicator we have built is positive (R = .104, p < .001), but still not too strong. The table 3.5 summarizes the correlations between social trust, membership in associations, and political attitudes and beliefs in Romania.

Regarding the data displayed in the tables above, we are unable to conclude with certainty that both social trust and membership in associations assist in supporting democratic attitudes, since the values of our measures are quite low and often not significant. The analysis still could demonstrate that democratic values are somehow related to social trust, but also to a particularized institutional trust, namely trust in democratic state institutions. People who participate in voluntary organizations are more trusting in other people and in state institutions, they are more oriented towards the political system and display a greater political competence. Moreover, they seem to embrace democratic values more than others do. But the overall effects of membership in voluntary associations are not so impressive, as it is generally claimed by the social capital theory. We cannot clearly determine the direction of causality in the relationships between membership, on one hand, and social and political trust, political interest and political competence, on the other hand. Although the civic activists are a hope for a future consolidation of the civil society and for a strong influence on the political system, we don't have yet any strong proof that they could become opinion leaders and pressure politicians and state institutions.

At this stage, we cannot fully explain the low level of membership in voluntary associations. However, the findings made by Howard (2003) in Russia and East Germany may be similar to those in Romania.

"As a result of the institutional experience of communism, with its forced mobilization and strict separation of public and private spheres (...) three main causal factors are responsible, and all three involve people's ongoing reinterpretations of prior and present experiences. These factors consist of 1. people's prior experiences with organizations, and particularly the legacy of mistrust of formal organizations that results from the forced participation in communist organizations, 2. the persistence of informal private networks, which function as a substitute or alternative for formal and public organizations, and 3. the disappointment with the new democratic and capitalist systems today, which has led many people to avoid the public sphere. Together, these three factors present an account of the causal link between people's interpretations of their prior experiences and their social behavior and activities today."

The same features could be pointed out in all post-communist countries. The overall conclusion is that civic participation is important for the spread of democratic values and the full consolidation of democracy in these countries, which were transitioning from authoritarian rule during the first decade of post-communism. A permanently weak civil society means that the democratic consolidation would depend merely on political elites and institutions and on the proper functioning of market economy. With economic crises that could affect large shares of ordinary citizens, the democratic commitment of political elites is decisive. We explore the importance of elite behavior when we tackle down the problem of populism in power. At this stage, the main finding is that low levels of social capital, which characterize ordinary citizens during early democratic transition, do not seriously hamper democratic consolidation by citizens' actions that would encourage or support non-democratic alternatives. In the same time, low levels of social capital could influence the general political participation, discouraging people in getting involved into political activity, as they generally do in civic activities. This may become a barrier for the consolidation of a democratic system where active and critical citizens interact with responsive and efficient political elites in solving political issues. This is the perspective we favor in the next chapter, dedicated to the political participation style.

3.4 Technical appendix

A statistical appendix figure here, at the end of this chapter, in order to clearly indicate how variables and scales have been used and constructed for statistical purposes. The exact phrasing of the questions used in the questionnaire is also present.

– The indicator of democratic attitudes:

For each of the following statements, can you tell me whether you agree strongly, agree, disagree or disagree strongly?

	Strongly agree	Agree	Disagree	Strongly disagree	DK/ NA
A55. Even it is not perfect, democracy is still the best form of government	4	3	2	1	9
D3. The president should – in fact – run the country	4	3	2	1	9
D4. Experts should – in fact – run the country and not political governments	4	3	2	1	9
D6. It would be better if the country were run by the military	4	3	2	1	9

The variables are added into a single index measuring democratic attitudes:

recode A55 (1,2=1) (else=0) into demo1.
recode D3 (4,3=1) (else=0) into demo2.
recode D4 (4,3=1) (else=0) into demo3.
recode D6 (4,3=1) (else=0) into demo4.
compute DEMO = demo1+demo2+demo3+demo4.

– The indicators of trust:

For each of the following statements, can you tell me whether you agree strongly, agree, disagree or disagree strongly?

	Strongly agree	Agree	Disagree	Strongly disagree	DK/ NA
B1. Most people can be trusted	4	3	2	1	9
B3. State institutions i.e., Parliament, Presidency, Government, Police and Judiciary system can be trusted	4	3	2	1	9
B4. The press can be trusted	4	3	2	1	9
B5. International organizations i.e., NATO or EU can be trusted	4	3	2	1	9

a. social trust:
recode B1 (1=1) (2,3=2) (4=3) (9=sysmiss) into SOCTRUST (1=low; 2=medium; 3=high).
b. trust in state institutions:
recode B3 (1=1) (2,3=2) (4=3) (9=sysmiss) into POLTRUST (1=low; 2=medium; 3=high).
c. institutional trust:
recode B4 (1=1) (2,3=2) (4=3) (9=sysmiss) into PRESTRUST (1=low; 2=medium; 3=high).
Recode B5 (1=1) (2,3=2) (4=3) (9=sysmiss) into ORGTRUST (1=low; 2=medium; 3=high).
Compute INSTRUST=POLTRUST+PRESTRUST+ORGTRUST.

- The indicators of civic attitudes:

For each of the following statements, can you tell me whether you agree strongly, agree, disagree or disagree strongly?

	Strongly agree	Somehow agree	Somehow disagree	Strongly disagree	DK/ NA
B6. People like me can do little or nothing to influence political events	4	3	2	1	9
B7. Political events have little or no impact on my life	4	3	2	1	9

B8. Could you tell me whether you are a member of a political party or political organization?

1. Yes   2. No   9. NA

B9. How interested would you say you are in politics?

4. Very interested   3. Somewhat interested   2. Not very interested
1. Not at all interested   9. DK/NA

How often do you...	Daily or almost daily	Several times a week	Several times a month	Never	DK/ NA
B10. Read political events in the newspapers?	3	2	1	0	9
B11. Watch political news on television?	3	2	1	0	9
B12. Discuss politics with family and/or friends?	3	2	1	0	9

B13. Did you vote in the latest elections (1996)?

1. Yes   2. No   8. This is not the case (had under 18 years)   9. DK/NA

a. impact of political events:
   recode B6 (4=1) (2,3=2) (1=3) (9=sysmiss) into POLIMPACT (1=low; 2=medium; 3=high).
b. influence on political events:
   recode B7 (4=1) (2,3=2) (1=3) (9=sysmiss) into POLINFL (1=low; 2=medium; 3=high).
c. political interest:
   recode B10 (9=sysmiss) (Else=copy) into POLPRESS.
   Recode B11 (9=sysmiss) (Else=copy) into POLTV.
   Recode B12 (9=sysmiss) (Else=copy) into DISCPOL.
   Compute POLINTER = POLPRESS+POLTV+DISCPOL.
– The membership in voluntary organizations:

Now I am going to read off a list of voluntary organizations; for each one, could you tell me whether you are a member of that type of organization?

Associations/organizations	Yes	No	NA
B15. Labor union	1	2	9
B16. Human rights organization	1	2	9
B17. Environment organization	1	2	9
B18. Sport association	1	2	9
B19. Professional association	1	2	9
B20. Charitable organization	1	2	9
B21. Religious organization (other than church)	1	2	9
B22. Any other voluntary organization	1	2	9

recode B15 (1=1) (else=0) into MEMB1.
Recode B16 (1=1) (else=0) into MEMB2.
Recode B17 (1=1) (else=0) into MEMB3.
Recode B18 (1=1) (else=0) into MEMB4.
Recode B19 (1=1) (else=0) into MEMB5.
Recode B20 (1=1) (else=0) into MEMB6.
Recode B21 (1=1) (else=0) into MEMB7.
Recode B22 (1=1) (else=0) into MEMB8.
Compute NUMBORG = MEMB1+MEMB2+MEMB3+MEMB4+MEMB5+ME
MB6+MEMB7+ MEMB8.
Recode NUMBORG (0=0) (else=1) into MEMBSHIP (0=No; 1=Yes).

– The responsiveness of the political personal:

Now I am going to read off a list of institutions. How do you consider they carry
out their duties and respond to people's demands?

	Very good	Fairly good	Fairly bad	Very bad	DK/ NA
A5. The Government	4	3	2	1	9
A6. The Parliament	4	3	2	1	9
A7. The Presidency	4	3	2	1	9
A20. The political opposition (parties in opposition)	4	3	2	1	9

recode A5 (9=sysmiss) (Else=copy) into GOVRESP
recode A6 (9=sysmiss) (Else=copy) into PARLRESP
recode A7 (9=sysmiss) (Else=copy) into PRESRESP
recode A20 (9=sysmiss) (Else=copy) into OPPRESP
compute POLRESP = GOVRESP+PARLRESP+PRESRESP+OPPRESP.

4 Social capital and political engagement in Romania

The conclusion of the previous chapter was that social capital had little or almost no impact on the support for democracy. Ordinary citizens generally reject the non-democratic alternatives, with only a small difference (statistically significant, but rather weak) for those who are more trustful and who are members in voluntary associations. A difference however has been noticed when it came to take into account civic attitudes, those who are related to citizens' political interest and political participation. This chapter therefore focuses on political participation and analyzes some of the reasons why political participation in Romania, although structurally comparable with other Western cases, is much weaker. Using data from another survey, this chapter tests for three main blocks of variables that are supposedly important for political participation, including human capital, economic resources and context variables, motivations and, finally, as the previous chapter stated, social capital variables. The analysis focuses on social capital factors, which are civic volunteerism and social trust. The conclusion is that, in fact, social capital is important for political activism and that civic activists may become, on the long run, a resource for effective mechanisms of control of political elites in Romania. They might help consolidate the public space, a space of freedom and dialogue, an environment where, following decades of terror and exclusion, people are free to express themselves without any coercion from any social or political authority.

Political participation is explored here in terms of civic engagement, protest and voting. In order to make the analysis of the Romanian case comparable with other country cases, we used the 2005–2006 World Values Survey dataset for Romania. This international comparative inquiry is a valuable and methodologically strong data source, generally used in aggregate analysis at country level. Case studies driven from this database are equally important for underlining the specific relationship between political activism and a range of essential factors in the post-communist settings. In the same time, this survey is part of a larger project financed by the Open Society Foundation, namely the Public Opinion Barometer (POB), a series of social and political surveys aimed at unravelling the public opinion change in Romania. The sample used here is composed of 1776 respondents, aged 18 years and more, which is representative for the Romanian adult population, with a calculated error of ± 2.3%.

Moving back to political engagement, the factors that we take into account here are three blocks of variables related to human capital, resources and context, motivations and social capital (volunteerism and social trust). The scholarly literature largely emphasizes the effects of participation in voluntary associations on political participation and the importance of trust for cooperation. As we underline here, political activism in Romania, although weaker than in Western societies, follows the same pattern as in Western settings (Barnes and Kaase 1979). Political activism still depends on motivations, namely on political interest and institutional confidence, on human capital variables, especially on education, and, finally, on social trust and volunteerism. This particular feature is of great importance for the consolidation of the public sphere. Membership in voluntary organizations may therefore become a general resource for cooperation that spills over society and teach the pursuit of the common interest.

We focus here only on the external effects of social capital. People active in voluntary associations might form organized civic groups that carry out specific actions of political communication (lobby, advocacy) and manage to control politicians in office. Such organized groups in civil society could force politicians to be more responsible, responsive and efficient by promising political support or by threatening those politicians with the withdrawal of the support. Citizens' response to such responsible behavior of politicians is a growing demand for valuable political solutions, which are at the same time accompanied by satisfaction, trust and partisanship moderation. This is the virtuous circle of modern democracy described by Putnam (1993) in his seminal work about how democracy works. The opposite is easy to imagine, that is alienated citizens and irresponsible, corrupt and indolent political elites. Therefore, people who participate in voluntary organizations in post-communist Europe could make a difference. They might form the democratic elite of organizational activists that are more trusting, tolerant and participatory, emphasize Bădescu, Sum and Uslaner (2004, 316). The cited authors view those individuals who are active in civil society as holding the greatest potential to form the yoke of democratic attitudes that might disseminate over time throughout society.

Bădescu, Sum and Uslaner (2004) have found that social capital level in Central and Eastern Europe is lower than in Western societies. There is no doubt that Central and Eastern European countries differ from the Western countries in respect of their recent past. If we don't consider trust as a psychological trait which may influence many aspects of later behavior, as Allport (1961) does, then we may consider the socializing conditions to be responsible for citizens' cooperation and commitment style. From this perspective, the present social connections come from the general constraints of the communist system, based on tight ideological control and mobilization, deletion and repression. Distrust, social atomization, and loose cooperation could all originate in the kind of connections people had in communist time (Völker and Flap 2001). Yet social and economic problems that citizens face now could be another factor explaining low levels of social capital in the region. Struggling through transition, people hardly find time to spend in company of friends, and have no time at all to spend for non-profit activities. Low levels of participation in voluntary organizations could be explained by the lack of resources, but also by the disappointing experience people have had with communist forced mobilization, the persistence of informal cooperation networks and, finally, by the frustration caused by the performance of the new democratic and economic system (Howard 2003).

4.1 The importance of political participation for democracy

Public opinion and researchers in Romania witnessed a vivid concern on public space issue, which is merely related to corruption outcomes (Uslaner and Bădescu 2004; Uslaner and Bădescu 2005; Uslaner 2007a). Corruption teaches the lesson of distrust and erodes social bonds, strengthens the powerless feelings among ordinary citizens and deepens inequality (Uslaner 2013). In turn, distrust consolidates corruption, fuels tax evasion, affects the legal system and makes inefficient governments to fail to provide essential services. In such an environment, people don't pay taxes as long as they don't believe that they will be treated fairly and equitably and when they believe that public officials steal their tax payments (Uslaner 2007b). The vicious circle leads to distrust and perceived inequity, on the one hand, and to inefficient, corrupt and indolent public officials (Mishler and Rose 2005). It seems that causal mechanisms work for many decades, significantly linking the access to mass education, economic equality and the control of corruption (Uslaner and Rothstein 2016). Moreover, there is a growing awareness regarding the issue on public sphere and cooperation (Preoteasa 2002). What seems to be lacking in Romania is a sense of community. In fact, Romanians cannot pursue the common interest because they don't have a common objective reality capable of supporting such a task. Instead of common objective reality, Romanians really have private interests that fully motivate them. When it comes to engaging in collective action, they cannot identify a common reality. They rather conceive a non-objective reality, which is elusive, remote, hostile, subject to manipulation by distant forces and impossible to change by ordinary citizens. This might explain why Romanian citizens generally turn out to be pessimistic and disengaged, as shown in Tabs. 4.1 to 4.5.

Tab. 4.1: The dimensions of political activism in Romania

	Civic activism	Protest	Voting
Membership political party	0,811		
Membership labor union	0,739		
Membership church or religious organization	0,685		
Membership sport or recreation organization	0,909		
Membership art, music or educational organization	0,908		
Membership environmental organization	0,949		
Membership professional associations	0,892		
Membership charitable organization	0,930		
Signing a petition		0,910	
Joining in boycotts		0,860	
Attending lawful demonstrations		0,898	
Voting in last elections			0,999
% variance	49.085	19.815	8.345

Factor analysis (Principal Component Analysis). Varimax rotation with Kaiser normalization. KMO = 0,921. N = 1776. Sig. = 0.001.

Tab. 4.2: Agreement with the free-riding behavior (egoism indicator)

Please tell me for each of the following statements whether you think it can always be justified (10), never be justified (1), or something in between, using this 1 to 10 scale	Mean	Standard deviation
Claiming state benefits which you are not entitled to	2,04	2,05
Travel by bus/train without paying a ticket (free-riding)	2,01	1,94
Cheating on tax if you have the chance	2,34	2,48
Someone accepting a bribe in the course of their duties	1,45	1,33

It is not easy to define the engagement in the public sphere, yet it is assumed that people activate in this public space by pursuing the common interest. The good citizen is interested in common matters and manages to overpass its narrow individual interest by willing to do one's shares in collective endeavors (Almond and Verba 1963). It seems that political participation is one of the few acts binding individuals in communities. Being politically active really means using one's citizenship and taking part in the common duties. In this vein, the first indicator of the willingness to engage in public sphere is to be politically active. In the terms of Verba, Schlozman and Brady (2000), political participation

Tab. 4.3: Factors influencing civic activism in Romania

	Resources, human capital and context model	Motivations model	Social capital model	Integrative model
Gender (male)	0.044			0.028
Age (continuous)	0.061			0.071*
Education (1-14)	0.130***			0.123**
Urban residence	-0.092**			-0.113***
Full-time job	0.128***			0.121***
Church attendance (1-7)	0.067*			0.045
Socio-economic status (1-5)	0.038			0.059
Household income (continuous)	0.064			0.062
Positive about household economic situation in one year (1-5)	0.012			-0.008
Positive about current economic system (1-5)	0.005			-0.012
Control over one's own life (1-10)	0.020			0.041
Political interest		0.127***		0.083**
Trust in democratic institutions		0.027		0.018
Agreement with free-riding behavior		0.106***		0.070*
Social trust			-0.004	-0.017
Adj. R Square	0.059	0.027	-0.001	0.072

Regression analysis (OLS). * p < 0.05, ** p < 0.01, *** p < 0.001. Entries in the table above are standardized coefficients (Beta).

means more than voting, but incorporates all acts that are intended to have the consequence of influencing the choice of governing officials or the policies they make and implement. Political participation has been evolving from simple, conventional forms (voting and working for political parties) to new, unconventional forms, that is protest (Barnes and Kaase 1979). Alongside conventional forms, participation in volunteer associations is another type of participation.

Political activity in Western Europe changed during decades of economic, social and political development, following World War II, into unconventional

Tab. 4.4: Factors influencing protest in Romania

	Resources, human capital and context model	Motivations model	Social capital model	Integrative model
Gender (male)	0.072*			0.026
Age (continuous)	0.086**			0.084*
Education (1-14)	0.110**			0.109*
Urban residence	-0.002			0.009
Full-time job	0.083*			0.067*
Church attendance (1-7)	-0.008			-0.043
Socio-economic status (1-5)	-0.019			-0.026
Household income (continuous)	0.137***			0.133***
Positive about household economic situation in one year (1-5)	-0.058			-0.072*
Positive about current economic system (1-5)	-0.010			-0.015
Control over one's own life (1-10)	-0.007			-0.032
Political interest		0.169***		0.102**
Trust in democratic institutions		0.020		0.059
Agreement with free-riding behavior		-0.012		-0.017
Social trust			0.009	0.014
Volunteerism			0.145***	0.111***
Adj. R Square	0.051	0.028	0.020	0.079

Regression analysis (OLS). * $p < 0.05$, ** $p < 0.01$, *** $p < 0.001$. Entries in the table above are standardized coefficients (Beta).

forms. In the industrial period, with social structure and with growing alternatives in ideologies, political parties and movements, people developed loyalties to those ideologies, parties and movements in order to acquire guidance in how to think and act politically (Barnes 2004a). According to Barnes (2004a), a new type of mobilization emerged and replaced the previous political mobilization, in accordance with the changes in values going on in the world (Inglehart 1977, 1990). The emerging age is one of cognitive mobilization. Although many people

Tab. 4.5: Factors influencing voting in Romania

	Resources, human capital and context model	Motivations model	Social capital model	Integrative model
Gender (male)	0.048			0.001
Age (continuous)	0.056			0.058
Education (1-14)	0.023			0.013
Urban residence	-0.049			-0.021
Full-time job	0.038			0.026
Church attendance (1-7)	0.114***			0.087*
Socio-economic status (1-5)	-0.031			-0.050
Household income (continuous)	0.018			0.011
Positive about household economic situation in one year (1-5)	0.031			-0.005
Positive about current economic system (1-5)	-0.027			0.027
Control over one's own life (1-10)	0.097**			0.083*
Political interest		0.089**		0.064*
Trust in democratic institutions		0.100***		0.099*
Agreement with free-riding behavior		-0.073**		-0.062*
Social trust			0.017	0.013
Volunteerism			0.047*	0.023
Adj. R Square	0.023	0.026	0.001	0.041

Regression analysis (OLS). * p < 0.05, ** p < 0.01, *** p < 0.001. Entries in the table above are standardized coefficients (Beta).

remain tied to the political system in the older social and political patterns of adherence, in the age of generalized education and mass communication, there is less need to turn to parties for guidance on public policy. Now people are free to choose among a vast range of causes, civil society associations and solicitations and they do so in terms of personal interests and passions. There has been a growing acceptance of what were once considered to be unconventional forms of political action. Today, protest politics fits well with social movements' patterns of political activity and with the changes in civil society and parties (Norris, Walgrave and van Aelst 2005).

4.2 Political activism and its essential factors

Political activism is the dependent variable in this chapter. When we look at the political activism in Romania, we find that it clearly follows the path unraveled in the '70s by Barnes and Kaase (1979) and splits into distinctive patterns of political activity, namely into voting, membership in secondary organizations and protest. While civic activism includes the membership in various secondary organizations, such as political parties, labor unions and religious, educational, sport, charitable, professional, environmental organizations, protest includes activities as signing a petition, joining in boycotts and attending lawful demonstrations. In order to clearly measure civic activism and protest, we build scales by adding the related items in the questionnaire. Each of these dimension scales of political activism proves to be fully reliable (the reliability analysis indicates a Crombach's Alpha measure of 0.9366 for the civic activism scale and of 0.8671 for the protest scale).

People participate in politics because they can, because they want or because they were asked to (Verba, Schlozman and Brady 2000). Therefore, the independent variables we have selected are grouped in three main blocks, namely resources, human capital and context variables, motivation variables and finally, social capital. Those are the variable blocks which we use in order to explain political participation.

People with higher household income, those who feel more positive about their household economic situation and more positive about the current economic system are more likely to be politically active. At the same time, human capital might be of great importance: age, education, control over one's own life, gender and socio-economic status might influence one's disposition in participating. We actually draw these variables from a test made by Rose and Weller (2003) on essential conditions for democracy in Russia. The Russian context is largely comparable to the Romanian one, therefore we use here the same measures for economic resources and human capital. We add some other context variables, which we expect to influence political participation, namely the urban residence, the church attendance and the full-time job. They are generally used in electoral analysis, where they prove important for the way people decide upon candidates.

Motivations are the second block of variables we have to take into account in order to assess what factors influence political participation. People might be discouraged to participate by their own orientation towards the political system. Political interest may be seen somehow as a prerequisite for political participation. Another factor that could discourage people to participate is their low trust in the political system. It seems useless to participate when you have no hope to influence political institutions. These institutions are generally seen as rigged against ordinary people and run by corrupt and irresponsible officials. Trust in democratic institutions is seen as a key element for the democratic legitimacy and the support for the democratic regime (Dalton 1999; Newton and Norris 2000). Therefore, we measure people's confidence in the representative institutions of democracy (parliament, presidency, political parties and mayoralties) in order to estimate their institutional trust.

People generally abstain from engaging in political activities when they cannot identify the common interest with other people (Bădescu, Sum and Uslaner 2004, 325). We already pointed out that public space is related to the definition of the common interest and we have acknowledged that defining common interest in not an easy task at all. Yet common interest might be defined at large as the willingness to cooperate and to refrain from egoism. Following Stolle and Rochon (1998), we consider the rejection of free riding as a proxy for altruism and, respectively, the approval of free riding as a proxy for egoism. In fact, what it is important is that approving the free riding mainly expresses a lack of concern regarding the consequences of one's acts for his fellow citizens. In this vein, World Values Survey questionnaires contain items designed to record such condemnation of free riding. By adding those items, we build a scale of egoism that proves to be reliable for our analysis (Crombach's Alpha = 0.8057).

In the operationalization of altruism, we closely follow Stolle and Rochon (1998), who have designated a wide range of attitudinal variables as important for social capital. The approval of free riding is one of these variables, along with tolerance and optimism. According to Stolle and Rochon (1998, 52), social capital also implies a willingness to do one's shares in collective endeavors. In a setting rich in social capital, one is less likely to expect others to be free riders and, partly in consequence, one is also less likely to be a free rider. Voluntary associations might probably teach this public ethic of condemning the free riding in the use of public services and other associated behaviors, such as lying or stealing a car. All these inappropriate behaviors have in common the fact that they disregard others' interests and persons, that they do not take into account the plausible consequences of one's acts for other people. Knack and Keefer (1997) also consider that norms of reciprocity are defined by attitudes of cooperation with strangers in prisoner dilemma settings. Civic cooperation is generated by people's willingness to cooperate when confronted with an issue related to collective action. That is why van Schaik (2002) uses the rejection of free-riding as a proxy for reciprocity norms.

Despite social capital has no official definition, there is a minimum consensus that its main components are social trust and membership in voluntary associations. The question related to social trust in the World Values Survey questionnaire is: 'Generally speaking, would you say that most people can be trusted or that you can't be too careful in dealing with people?' When compared, citizens in Eastern European countries display less trust in most people than citizens of West European countries generally do. Bădescu (2003a) discovered that the mean proportion of trustworthy persons is higher in consolidated West European democracies than in the former communist countries. The difference could be real, yet it could come from the meaning of "people". Bădescu emphasizes that a better operationalization would be ethnic trust. In fact, Uslaner and Conley (2003) unraveled different effects of generalized and particularized (and ethnic) trust in the case of American communities. Integrated and diverse neighborhoods lead to higher levels of trust, especially if people have also diverse social networks, whereas residential segregation leads to lower levels of social trust (Uslaner 2010).

As mentioned in our chapter dedicated to social capital, another problem raised by social trust is its relationship with institutional trust. It is important to know what are the linkages between the two types of trust, because they may affect the overall statistical model of reliability. Once again, there is no consensus regarding this relationship. While Norris (1999) considers the influence running from interpersonal to institutional trust, Brehm and Rahn (1997) depict the relationship as circular. At the same time, Newton (2001) doubts about any relationship between the two types of trust. For him, social trust and political (or institutional) trust are two different dimensions. They tend to be expressed by different kinds of people for different sorts of reasons. In our statistical model, we also take the two types of trust as expressing different realities and consider them unrelated.

Participation in voluntary organizations is commonly seen as related to the interpersonal trust, while the latter is an important ingredient for cooperation. Even when there are solid confirmations of the relationship between voluntary participation and trust (Wollebaek and Selle 2002), other scholars continue to be skeptical about it. The correlation between the two variables one can find in various surveys may be, in fact, the consequence of a selective recruitment of the participants in secondary organizations. Their members are exactly those who trust other people, whereas people who display less trust are not to be found between the members of such organizations. Even when one can find a positive correlation between those variables, the relationship is rather weak, statistically speaking. Newton (1999) discovered that it is inconsistent at country aggregate level. Even in theory, emphasizes the author, there are few arguments in favor of this relationship. The time one spends in the organization is incomparably more reduced than that spent in other socializing environments, as family, school, workplace or neighborhood. Secondly, there are other factors that already proved important for trust and civic engagement, education for example, as pointed out by Almond and Verba (1963).

4.3 Explaining low political activism in post-communist Romania

Although participation in Romania fits with the Western pattern of activity dimension, it largely contrasts by its low intensity. Various scholars studying Romanian society noticed this feature (Bădescu, Sum and Uslaner 2004; Sum 2005; Uslaner and Bădescu, 2004). In fact, Romanian low political participation is part of a general tendency in post-communist Europe (Barnes 2004b; Howard 2002b). People participate in politics because they can, because they want or because they were asked to. Therefore, Verba, Schlozman and Brady (2000, 246) explain the low political participation in terms of lack of resources (time, money, skills needed for political activity), motivations (interest for politics, preferences for particular policies, other gratification that might come from political activity) and recruitment. This is quite the same in post-communist Europe, emphasize various scholars (Bădescu, Sum and Uslaner 2004; Uslaner 2004; Uhlin 2010). One should not neglect the social shock in transforming Central and Eastern Europe. Erosion and the collapse of the social safety net and the rise of permanent unemployment and poverty took the society surprise, reminds us Berend (2007). Living standards declined; thus people became lacking in resources, enabling them to participate politically. At the same time, after 1989, people feel politically powerless and disregard public issues. They reject mobilization because they still remember the communist kind of party-state mobilization. Thus, post-communist participation seems to be much more dependent of communist legacy than previously thought, in terms of civic engagement (Pop-Eleches and Tucker 2013) and trust in state institutions (Dimitrova-Grajzl and Simon 2010; Howard 2003).

Another legacy of post-communism is the wide range of social (personal) networks, specific to atomized societies, that make such more formal civil society organizations to be unattractive for many people (Gibson 2003). Even when they were largely useful in time of political stress during the communist era (Völker and Flap 2001), personal networks survival is an anti-modern mark and a burden for the consolidation of today civil society. The persistence of networks has turned into a response to the organization failure and to the corruption of formal organizations (Leipnik 2013). Networks that individuals can invoke in response are anti-modern: forms of informal, diffuse social cooperation, begging or cajoling public officials, using connections to 'bend' rules or paying bribes that break rules (Rose 1998). These pre-modern social features, non-official kinship and networking organizations, survived in post-communism and were ready-made networks for corruption in the new post-communist settings. "Skillful use of connections, friends and relatives in the rights positions, and bribes guaranteed the required inside information to enable a go-getter to be first in line for an unprecedented opportunity (…) Corruption became an element of the political and economic system" (Berend 2007, 279). Growing informal economies in the region during the post-communist transition may fuel both perceptions of corruption and loss of trust in public institutions (Wallace and Latcheva 2006).

We test here the relationship between features of social capital, namely trust and reciprocity, and political participation in Romania, by comparing its effects with those of other variables, which are people's resources and motivations. The three tables above present the impact of three blocks of independent variables on the three dimensions of political activity, taken separately.

4.3.1 The impact of resources, human capital and context variables

Looking at the regression models grouping resources, human capital and context variables, one can easily notice the differences and similarities between political activities. While human capital proves to be of some importance for civic activism and protest through variables such as gender, age and especially education, it has no importance for voting. Having a full-time job has an impact on protest and civic activism, but not on voting. Household income is surprisingly unimportant for civic activism, but seems to be important for protest. This later political activity, protest, has been growing faster in Western capitalist Europe in the 1970s, largely driven by the rise of post-material values (Inglehart 1977). Thus it is not surprising to see that young people take to the streets of great Western cities but also engage into more traditional politics (Norris, Walgave and van Aelst 2005). Uslaner (2004, 4) doubts that Romanian protesters are driven by post-material values, since Romania discovered the material benefits of capitalism only recently. Protesters are indeed young, but not necessarily the best educated, the most civically active, the avant-garde of activism towards a better world. They are rather facing future with pessimism and withdrawal and are not the same people taking part in conventional politics. They belong to unions more than to civic groups. It is possible, indeed, that protesters in Romania are organized by labor unions. At this stage, let us emphasize that protest has changed from the 2005–2006 World Values Survey, with a new generation taking in the streets of big cities in Romania, protesting for environmental and various political causes. They seem nowadays to differ more and more from the more conventional participants, being successfully mobilized through new communication facilities.

Voting is influenced only by the belief that one is in control over what happens to himself and by the church attendance. While the first predictor might be related to the belief that people hold a degree of political power in influencing elected officials, that they are not powerless in partially shaping public policies by promising their votes and threatening with their withdrawal, the second predictor, namely the church attendance, is more ambiguous. Church attendance has an impact on civic activism and on voting. Whereas the first effect might be explained by membership in church or other religious organizations, the second effect might be caused by political mobilization. People attending the church could be politically mobilized by priests, especially in rural communities, and vote more frequently than other people. At the same time, they tend to be older, less educated and more rural, so there is a circularity in the regression model that might overestimate the church attendance's impact. But the three political activities have in common a very low fraction of their variance explained by resources, human capital and context variables.

4.3.2 The impact of motivation variables

When variables expressing motivation are introduced in the regression models, one can notice that they do not explain more of the variance of political activities than the previous block of variables (expressing resources, human capital and the context). But motivations are somehow important for political participation, especially political interest, which influence all three kinds of political activity.

Trust in democratic institutions is important only for voting, yet this is an essential feature. Voting is not only a civic right, but it is also a regulation mechanism, one way citizens may influence the political system. We will emphasize its importance when we discuss about populists' attempt to postpone elections. Free and fair voting procedures may favor institutional trust on the long run. It may favor the citizens' confidence that political institutions do not abuse their position of power, in this case in manipulating the voting procedures. Two competing theories, the cultural and performance explanation, proved to be important for institutional trust when tested in Eastern Europe (Lühiste 2006; Mishler and Rose 2005). Trust in other people and the confidence in the functioning of the economic and political system both influence citizens' institutional trust.

The agreement with free-riding is equally important for civic activism and for voting, but in different ways. While the agreement with the free-riding behavior inhibits people voting, it seems to help civic activism, which is at least unexpected and strange. We expected to see a different impact of reciprocity, which is a positive correlation between the rejection of free-riding and participation in voluntary organizations. This unexpected feature brings new questions about civic activism in Romania.

4.3.3 The impact of social capital

The explanatory power of social capital is generally weak. Social capital merely explains two percent of the variance of protest and explains virtually nothing of the overall civic activism and voting in Romania. It is quite scant when compared to the expectations of the social capital theory. Yet it is noticeable that civic activism and protest are related, contrary to what Uslaner (2004) has found in his research concerning political participation in Romania. And the relationship still holds on in the integrative model that takes into account the influence of all three blocks of variables. People who decide to be civic activists are those who engage more frequently in protest activities, meaning that protest mobilization is done by people already active in voluntary associations. With a limited number of people involved in voluntary associations, civic activists might use protest as a pressure tool for elected officials, only to return at their voluntary activities once the protest is ready. This feature is to be seen in the latest events in Romania, when civic activists managed to mobilize in January 2017 numerous protesters against the newly elected parliamentary majority and the PSD government it supported.

The integrative regression models for all three dimensions of political participation unravel that resources, especially education, are important for all types of political activity, except voting, and most notably for civic activism. This is not a novelty. It only confirms numerous findings in both Western and Eastern Europe (Almond and Verba 1963; Verba, Schlozman and Brady 2000; Bădescu 2003a; Uslaner 2004). But motivations are equally important, especially when regarding political interest. Trust in democratic institutions seems to motivate people only for voting, while rejecting the free-riding does the same. Social capital proves to be an ingredient for protest by its civic activism component alone, but its overall effect is weaker than expected.

Although social capital's impact is weaker than one would have expected, we notice that it is still important. Although its impact is meager on voting, civic activism proves to be a resource for protest. This is in line with classical findings and of great importance for democracy in Romania. In fact, civic activism seems to spill over and help political protest. Cooperation is, indeed, the key for effective pressure on the political establishment in the aim of citizens' strong influence on public issues. Civic activists might promote trust, dialogue and cooperation, but also help generate political resources that citizens need in order to control irresponsible political elites. As underlined before, political participation is essential for democracy because it links citizens and elected officials in an input-output system. Therefore, it is vital that societies in the region generate a democratic mechanism of controlling political elites. According to the theory of political control (Putnam 1993; Rose-Ackerman 2007; Uslaner 2007a; Warren 1999), effective linkages between citizens and politicians are the key to political and economic performance (Kluegel and Mason 2004). With no political participation, with no leverage of control, citizens are at the mercy of political elites and can only hope for accidental honest and responsible elites. With no citizens' control, there is no reason to believe that political elites would desire indeed to behave in an honest, responsible and decent manner. On the contrary, one could expect only to find corruption, bad management, poor economic performance, public discontent and a general feeling of powerlessness in such a polity. In the long run, elites could consolidate their power and rule by violence and fear alone. These are the virtuous and vicious circles plausibly linking citizens and political elites.

Associations could become in Romania schools of democracy, teaching trust and cooperation and civic activists might even become an example for society and play the function of opinion leaders (Bădescu, Sum and Uslaner 2004, 340). They might be the first to break the vicious circle of corruption, distrust, lack of interest and disengagement from public action, especially when people who perceive government as corrupt and untrustworthy tend to invest trust in civil organizations, namely in NGOs and charity organizations (Marinova 2011). Since they don't seem to strongly reject free-riding, these findings make us question the internal effects of voluntary participation. In fact, participation in voluntary associations might prove not to be enough for teaching the habits of cooperation and trust. As underlined by Bădescu, Sum and Uslaner (2004, 338), average membership length is less than two years in Romania. If activists stay active only for two years, stress the authors, this democratic advance guard may drop out of civic life and become as mistrusting as other citizens. Moreover, according to the authors, many associations in Romania seem in the 1990s to have heavily relied on Western funds and taken much of their organizational initiative from Western sources. They actually have much more to do with international available funding that with local needs (Howard 2003). In the long run, they rely more on paid members than on volunteers. Such NGOs even turn little by little into private public offices, which cannot address to the real local needs and that stop working when the available foreign funding stops. This feature may explain the unexpected correlation between membership in voluntary organizations and the approval of free-riding in our survey.

But our interest is not limited to political activism. There is a hope that civic activists in Romania might become politically active and help in the rebirth of a public sphere, a space of freedom and dialogue, an environment where people are free to express themselves without any coercion from any social or political authority. Those expectations have been fulfilled, at least partially, as we unravel in the following chapters, by a changing of generations and participation style. Activism in voluntary associations, clubs and congregations has not only internal effects. Civic activism not only teaches participants the lesson of democracy by generating a space of debating and decision making, but it could spill over society itself. Civic activism fosters political activism by his lessons of cooperation and pursuit of the common interest. Many NGO members have become politically active after 2014, founding political parties and working for a change in the leadership style, by condemning the pervasive corruption of established political parties and offering alternatives. By consolidating trust between individuals with different social, religious and ethnic backgrounds, social capital facilitates cooperation on a larger social scale. Post-communist societies desperately need to rebuild a public space with its incumbent political function, that is to put the decision-makers to account (Mzavanadze 2009). In this vein, public space is a medium for political justification, as well as for political initiative and political support. In any given polity, this is the common good of citizens and perhaps, the only common good they have, because public space is the depository of the common interest. And social capital, political performance and political support are mutually inter-dependent (Newton 2005), with participatory citizens putting politicians to account, yet offering to the democratic regime the support it requires for a proper functioning.

5 Social dependency and predatory elites: from state capture to external conditionality

The hope for a participatory citizenry is important when one takes into account the more stable, heavy factors that influence democratization. No perspective on democratic process is complete without focusing on those structural factors. They relate to basic structures that shape the economic development and the configuration of power elites. As mentioned earlier, the combination of the two main perspectives adopted here (*path-dependency theory* and the *competition theory*) lead to such factors that seriously influence democratization. Power elites generally compete for resources that enable them to thrive in various social and political system configurations. They influence the institutional design and get involved in the regulation of the economic process. That is why we decided to emphasize in this chapter the important role they play for democratization.

The openness of the democratic system, its stability and consolidation do not rely exclusively on the political style of the citizens, but on the commitment of political elites, as well. In fact, political elites are themselves embedded in the process of democratization by their role in forging institutions and stabilizing economies. Their attitudes toward democracy are critical (Evans and Whitefield 1995; Rogowski 1974). Although institutional trust is important for democratization (Newton and Norris 2000), its relationship with other forms of trust is not fully explained. That is why we do not focus here, in the second half of this volume, on institutions as objects of trust among citizens, but on elites' behavior and its impact of the general process of democratization. In other words, we take elites as key actors that shape democratization in accordance with their specific interests.

When the public support for democracy is weak, power elites could more easily transform the regime, sliding towards authoritarianism with no public protest. It was the case of the coup in Argentina in 1966 (Dahl 1971), but is the case of many current hybrid regimes. One should not forget that in the early stages of democratization the outcome of the competition between elites could lead to democratization, as it could lead to a backslide towards authoritarianism, or keep the country in a long-lasting status-quo (Ekman 2009; Haerpfer 2008; McFaul 2002). At the same time, political elites are embedded in the process of transforming the former socialist economies and their participation is not free of any individual or group interests (Stark and Bruzt 1998). Corruption, self-interest and non-democratic attitudes could heavily influence the way elites behave during democratization, with an emphasis put on the changing and unstable trajectories of new democratic states in the region. As unraveled in the current and following chapters, democratization is not a short period process. This is especially true for the hybrid regimes Ukraine and Moldova, where both citizens and political elites are undecided, balancing between post-Soviet semi-authoritarianism and democratic openness, between Soviet nostalgia and the faith into Western integration (Kuzio 2005; Munro 2007; Tudoroiu 2011). With the help of shifting elites, many citizens in post-Soviet countries still evaluate the impact of social transformations during transition by fostering a Soviet nostalgia (Mazur 2015). This is especially true today, when Russia itself managed to find a way of getting out from the former communist regime settings and continue modernization under new circumstances, but keeping alive the memory of good old days (Dawisha 2005). The current Russian modernization, away from the model of liberalization of market economy and full democratization, but conceived as the revival of a great power based on its own political culture (Kivinen and Cox 2016), is today an alternative to the more classical post-communist transition experienced by countries from Central and Eastern Europe. Based on a different paradigm than the Western democratic model, Russian modernization is taken into account by citizens from other post-Soviet republics. Following apparently decisive steps towards consolidation, many regimes proved weaker than expected. Even in Central and Eastern Europe, especially in Hungary and Poland, political elites turned back towards more authoritarian leadership style or towards the concentration of the executive power, in the framework of a direct democracy. Speaking for the people lead therefore to more executive power and to undemocratic provisions regarding citizens and parties in the opposition. This is also partially true for Romania, as we will emphasize later on.

For the moment, let us focus on the relationship between elites and citizens in the early stages of the democratic transition. With high expectations regarding democratization, the incipient and inchoate civil society found itself facing reluctant political elites. The first cleavage to be noticed in Romanian post-communist politics is between more active citizens supporting reforming the state, pushing for economic transformations and favoring a more critical approach towards the communist past, on the one hand, and the new political elites who inherited the legacy on the communist power structure (Pop-Eleches 1999), National Salvation Front (Frontul Salvării Naţionale – FSN). The anti-communist cleavage is thus defining for the first years of transition, when communist successor parties, willing to accommodate economic reform and political transition with moderate social costs, found themselves under the pressure of the civil society and opposition parties (Mihuţ 1994; Tănăsoiu 2008; Tismăneanu 1993). FSN soon split in half, giving birth to the Social Democracy Party (Partidul Democraţiei Sociale din România – PDSR), later on the Social Democrat Party (Partidul Social Democrat – PSD), and to the Democrat Party (Partidul Democrat – PD), later on the Democrat Liberal Party (Partidul Democrat Liberal – PDL). In the first years of transition, PDSR was targeted as the main communist successor party and accused not only for delaying severe economic measures, but for opposing to the lustration of the former communist party members.

Counting on numerous former communist party officials, entrenched in the state apparatus and the state economic structures, made PDSR unwilling to seriously tackle the issue of criminalizing the political past activities of its members. This led to only limited access to the former secret police (*Securitate*) files, and made impossible the moral cleansing of politics and society, with all the subsequent frustration of the opposition and of the incipient civil society (Ciobanu 2009; Stan 2002). The very sensitive issue of the access to the *Securitate* files (Stan 2004) triggered a controversy related to the individual and collective guilt of the former members of the former communist party officials, slowly deriving from the penal prosecution of those found guilty (very few people), to the moral condemnation of the communist ideology, put in practice by many people (Dragoman 2014). More specifically, the exclusion of the priests from the list of those investigated by the "truth commission" in charge of unravelling the secrets of the former secret police kept alive the suspicion regarding the willingness of the former clergy to cooperate with state authorities in various matters (Stan and Turcescu 2005; Turcescu and Stan 2015). All in all, the debate led to no practical issues, since Romania did not embrace the transitional justice methods adopted by some of its neighbors (Appel 2005; Killingsworth 2010; Stan 2012). It only strengthened the public domination of liberal ideas, by inhibiting the critique of left-wing intellectuals (Dragoman 2015b) and thus turning neo-liberalism as the only game in town. With the change in government and the coming of right-wing parties in power beginning with 1997, Romania engaged in the path of large scale privatization and full marketization. However, the unconditional support of right-wing intellectuals for right-wing parties in power had a critical impact on the consolidation of populism following the 2007 accession of Romanian to the European Union, as emphasized later on in this volume.

5.1 Social dependency, state-led violence and post-communist elites

The tensions derived from the anti-communist cleavage shaped the configuration of the political space for decades, with the communist successor parties aligning to the left and the anti-communist parties to the right side of the political spectrum. The opposition to PDSR was made by a large array of smaller parties, grouped under the umbrella of a political coalition labeled the Democratic Convention (Convenția Democratică din România – CDR). The most prominent parties from inside CDR were the National Liberal Party (Partidul Național Liberal – PNL) and the National Peasant Christian-Democrat Party (Partidul Național Țărănesc Creștin-Democrat – PNȚCD). The opposition formed by CDR was strengthened by PD, a faction split from FSN, as well as by the Democratic Alliance of the Hungarians (Uniunea Democrată a Maghiarilor din România – UDMR). The divide was strengthened by generational and cultural changes, with more educated and urbanized young people voting on the right-wing and publically pushing for quick and deeper reforms of the former communist economy and state. On the other side, successor parties, and especially PDSR (PSD later on), benefited of the support of less educated and less urbanized voters. They were mainly peasants and workers, living in rural areas and medium and small towns, who suffered the most from the brutal change of economic structures and social conditions. One should not underestimate the social shock triggered by the massive change of property, economic structure and employment qualification standards. The fading social safety net and the new market standards for getting employed, combined with the declining living standards, social deprivation and uncertainty (Berend 2007), made large shares of voters to look for parties that at least offered a better prospect for their future.

One might say that those electors got captive to those political parties' interests and policies, which worked out in strengthening their dependency. In parallel, those parties captured the state by their local elites (Mungiu-Pippidi 2003), making thus dependency work. By providing those electors from remote, backward rural areas with state aids in cash or in various types of goods (coal or wood for heating during winter time, e.g.), those parties were restating a severe dependency, echoing the latifundism that economically dominated the region before World War I (Lubecki 2004). The regions where agricultural proletarians and impoverished peasants experienced communism as an unprecedented social advancement are those which support stronger the communist successor parties. This is a solid explanation why those people who suffered the most during transition, those who maybe largely overemphasize today the good old days of the socialist regime (Hofferbert and Klingemann 2001), support the successor parties and respond to their promises. Combined with the state capture that accompanied state building following the dismantling of the previous communist political and economic system (Grzymala-Busse 2007), including privatization of valuable assets previously owned by the state and colonizing state administration, the action of political elites in power may sound as pessimistic as the "theft of a nation" (Gallagher 2005). This is especially the case when state capture is accompanied by the limitation (or at least the permanent intention to limit) of the political resources of the opposition and the repression of overt contention. Fearing the spread of the contention triggered by the protests of the opposition parties during the spring of 1990, FSN encouraged his supporters to take to the streets, as a counterstrike aimed to consolidate FSN in power. Some of these supporters, probably the most violent, were coal miners. They organized in the Jiu Valley, an important coal basin in Romania, and moved by train several times to Bucharest, with the acknowledgment if not the formal approval of FSN government (Gledhill 2005). Their savage riot in Bucharest in June 1990 ended with squatting of the University Square, the place that the opposition parties used for demonstration, as well as with the devastation of opposition parties' headquarters. The coal miners' actions were publically praised by the President of Romania, former FSN leader, Ion Iliescu. Moreover, the "fist of the working class" (Vasi 2004) is to be used once again in September 1991, when the government led by Petre Roman was toppled down by the brutal coal miners siege of the parliament. The successive venues of coal miners to Bucharest, as well as the reluctance of the governing party to take serious steps in transforming the state and the economy plunged the country into political isolation. At that moment, one would have hardly believed that any factor would be effective in putting Romania back on track again.

5.2 Democratization under external control

The pessimism expressed by the opposition parties and the incipient civil society in those years during early transition was slowly lifted by the democratic trajectory of the country. Looking back, Romania's trajectory was different from that of other post-communist countries. On the one hand, it was different from that of countries from Central Europe, and this difference aroused the pessimistic views of the opposition and of several scholarly researchers (Roper 2000; Tismăneanu 1993). Hungary, Poland, Slovakia and the Czech Republic made decisive steps towards democratization and above all marketization (Fish and Choudhry 2007), benefitting of external aid under the form of direct investments and development funding. The European Union PHARE programme was initially destined to support Hungary and Poland's development efforts, only to be later on extended to other EU candidate countries. On the other hand, Romania was far from the violence triggered by dismantling the former Soviet Union and former Yugoslavia (Ramet 2002). Despite the ethnic tensions that brought Romania at the brink of the ethnic civil war in March 1990, due to bloody ethnic clashes between ethnic Hungarians and ethnic Romanians in Târgu-Mureş, a town in the heart of Transylvania, political and economic transition was not severely affected by statehood and nationhood problems, as it was the case with the successor states of former Soviet Union and Yugoslavia. The latter had to solve the conflict between nation-building policies and more general policies aimed at crafting democracy (Linz and Stepan 1996). Their transition was more complicated because the newly democratic regimes, born on the ruins of the multi-national states, inherited from the previous communist regimes' serious problems, ranging from ethnic minorities and secessionist threats to violent border disputes (Kuzio 2001). Romania engaged into a totally different path of accommodating ethnic minorities and has become a model in solving ethnic disputes (Ram 2009).

External conditionality is to be conceived here as the willingness of the Romanian governing parties, with no exception, to comply with the European Union standards and requirements. Although external conditionality is not easy to unravel, since foreign affairs often combine with domestic politics, the EU accession of candidate countries is a good example of external conditionality. By setting up in 1993 a list of comprehensive conditions to fulfill for accession, known as the Copenhagen criteria, the European Commission sent a clear message regarding the requirements due to fulfill the common political, economic and administrative standards. Among political criteria, civil and human rights, as well as the respect for and protection of minorities, have become one of the most relevant issues when deciding starting negotiations with former communist states (Sasse 2004). In the area of minority rights, the EU conditionality worked in combination with the consolidation of democracy (Schimmelfennig 2007), aiming at fulfilling general requirements before starting technical negotiations with candidate countries for more specific matters (Pop-Eleches 2007; Schimmelfennig and Sedelmeier 2004; Tesser 2003). Compared with other negotiated policy domains, it seems that European conditionality was much more effective for minority issues. For example, the sub-national governance and the regional design (Dragoman and Gheorghiță 2016; John 2000; O'Dwyer 2006) have been much less affected.

The improvement of minority rights worked hand in hand with the general conditions for democratization, namely with reasonably free and fair elections, civil and political rights, and a rather free mass media. The reports issued by Freedom House, which measure the openness of the political system, stabilized at 2 on a scale from 1 to 7, where 1 is the most open and 7 the least open political system. In comparison, minority rights in Romania reached the European standards and sometimes overpassed them. This is the case with the European Charter for Regional or Minority Languages. Whereas Romania ratified the Charter in 2008, states like France and Italy signed the document without ratifying it, while other EU member states, like Greece, Belgium or Portugal, even refused to sign it (Căluşer 2009). Combined with the normative and political pressure of the Council of Europe and of the Organization for Security and Cooperation in Europe, the European Union accession criteria largely helped the unstable democracy in Romania (Ciobanu 2007).

A shift in minority rights conception in Romania was unconceivable without the changing political attitudes towards UDMR in Romania, as well as towards neighboring Hungarian state. Forming an opposition coalition with right-wing parties against PDSR between 1990 and 1996 (Mihailescu 2008), UDMR imposed as a key party in forming subsequent coalitions. Being part of governing coalitions gave UDMR a coalition potential that turned partially into a blackmail potential during the 1996–2000 period. It was the period when Romania made serious efforts, but finally failed to join NATO in 1999. In fact, the Romanian government expected that Romania would receive a formal invitation to join NATO at the organization's summit in Madrid. This was not the case, which put new pressure on the next government (2000-2004), formed by PSD with the essential support of UDMR in parliament.

The participation of the Hungarian party to the governing coalitions between 1996 and 2000 and the key party position in parliament between 2000 and 2004 fostered the favorable internal conditions for expanding linguistic rights for minorities (Chiribucă and Magyari 2003). In a contrasting shift from the previous period, minorities have been endowed with significant linguistic rights. Not only the very restrictive legal provisions in teaching history and geography have been lifted, but the use of minority languages was accepted at all educational levels, from primary school to the university level, with the obligation of teaching and learning Romanian as official language. Moreover, the use of minority languages was extended in justice matters and, very important, in public administration. The public debates in minority languages in the local councils were accepted, with proper translation in Romanian and with the final decision and disposition to be written in Romanian. According to the new Public Administration Law (No. 215 from 2001), in all localities where minorities trespass a 20% threshold, public institutions and local authorities use minority languages when in relation with citizens from minority groups. Finally, public inscriptions are equally provided in the minority language, wherever the minority group trespasses 20% of the population.

The current favorable minority rights are in deep contrast with the situation to be recorded during the first years of transition, when the settlement of a negotiated solution for minority rights combined with the general reshaping of the institutional design. Unlike other former communist states, as Hungary and Poland for example, which merely amended their former communist constitutions, Romania initiated a more complex procedure of writing a brand new democratic constitution that was to replace the obsolete communist one. Therefore, negotiations between ethnic Romanian and ethnic minorities elites regarded both the constitutional framework and specific laws on public administration and education in minority languages. Despite the openness for negotiating minority rights, the constitution adopted in 1991 generally reflects the willingness of the majority group to set up a dominant position. Romania was declared a national state whose sovereignty was based on the unity of the Romanian people, making thus a statement of dominance of the Romanian nation and language, which was adopted as the unique official language. Minority rights only come in second place, but they are clearly expressed as guaranteed by the constitution in the field of education, culture and religion, with the respect of the principle of equality and non-discrimination in relation to other citizens in Romania.

The protest response of Hungarian political elites in parliament reflected the disillusion for the inertia in changing ethnic Romanians' attitudes towards ethnic minorities. As one could have expected, the end of communism was about to bring a quick and undisputed improvement of minority status, making a difference from the previous era, when, in the final stages of communism, ethnic minorities felt under deep pressure from state authorities (Verdery 1995). At the same time, claims for cultural and administrative autonomy raised fears among ethnic Romanians, who still fear that larger autonomy for ethnic Hungarians could end in secession and open conflict, as it was then the case in former Yugoslavia. Those fears were largely exploited by parties in government, which were looking for alternative legitimacy issues in order to consolidate in power (Gallagher 2001). With the 1991 Constitution in place, the only room opened for improving the minority rights was negotiating specific laws on education and public administration, which were aimed at defining the cultural autonomy of ethnic minorities.

The Local Administration Act of 1991 reconfirmed the supremacy of the Romanian language, even in counties and localities where ethnic minorities constitute the majority of inhabitants. The law was so restrictive, that forced elected officials to use Romanian, the national language, in open debates in local councils, for example, even there was no ethnic Romanian elected official.

It went the same with official communications between local authorities and citizens, where minorities could use their native language in formal, written requests, only if they were accompanied by a Romanian translation. In practice, however, the Hungarian was much more used that regulated by the law, since public administration of those localities, where minorities were of significant importance, was considered an extension of the public space, where minorities were unrestrictedly speaking their own native language. The legal provisions were merely symbolic, aimed at clearly assessing the primacy of the Romanian language.

The same goes with education. Following a tense debate in parliament, the 1995 Act of Education was based on a rather narrow interpretation of the Constitution. Although the law acknowledged the use of Hungarian and other minority languages in primary, secondary and university education, it stated the obligation for disciplines as history or geography to be taught only in Romanian. This was a clear symbolic constraint, since it was well known that ethnic minorities use peculiar, different geographic denominations and that they use different perspectives when dealing with various historical events. This was of paramount importance for Romanian nationalists, since sharing the same geographic space with minorities (in Transylvania, for example) also means opposing conflicting historical narratives. It is worth mentioning that Romanian National Day, December the 1st, commemorates the 1918 attachment of Transylvania to modern Romania. At the same time, this attachment would have been impossible without a proper previous secession of the province from Austria-Hungary. Thus celebrating the National Day also means remembering to the Hungarians in Transylvania the loss of the province by the Hungarian state.

The case of minority rights sheds light on the effectiveness of external control. In the same time, in unravels a mechanism through which external conditionality may foster internal conditions for democratic consolidation. The ethnic crisis triggered by the Hungarian government in 2001 was overpassed with less damage than it would have happened only a decade before. It proves that European conditionality not only worked by imposing standards for minority rights, but it also helped to balance and stabilize political divergences and conflicts that could have occurred between ethnic groups or between neighboring states. The Council of Europe, and especially its Commission for Democracy, also known as the 'Venice Commission', helped the Romanian and the Hungarian governments to reach an agreement on the extra-territoriality of the support granted by the kin state to ethnic members living in neighboring states. By this, the Venice Commission tackled the discrimination effects of national laws, when they are designed to protect and support ethnic diaspora. It was exactly the case in 2001, when the Hungarian government issued a special Law on the Status of Hungarians Living in Neighboring Countries, also known as the 'Status Law'. The law was designed to support ethnic Hungarians living in the nearby diaspora, by granting them special rights like education, travel, working permits, social assistance and health benefits. Ethnic Hungarians were entitled to the benefit of those facilities in Hungary, as well as at home, in the neighboring countries. In fact, the law not only aimed to facilitate their stay on the Hungarian territory (museum and library tickets, bus tickets, other discounts and facilities), but to support ethnic Hungarians living in the near diaspora to use their native language (monthly allocations for children attending Hungarian language schools and universities). Equally symbolic and practical, the 'Status Law' was in fact expanding the Hungarian nation (Deets 2006; Kulcsár and Bradatan 2007), by turning Hungarian diaspora into a political actor in Hungarian politics (Batory 2010; Fowler 2004; Rajacic 2007; Waterbury 2006).

The 'Status Law' excited much criticism from all the neighboring states, and the Hungarian government decided to adopt the recommendations of the 'Venice Commission', by amending the law. During negotiations with the governments of the neighboring states, especially with the Romanian government run by PSD, the Hungarian government limited the application of the law on the Hungarian soil alone and eliminated the discriminatory provisions in granting the working permits and other kinds of support. Moreover, the certificates confirming the status of beneficiaries as ethnic Hungarians were to be issued and distributed by the Hungarian state itself, with no support from the Hungarian associations in neighboring countries. The compromise accepted by the Hungarian government, under the supervision of the Council of Europe's Commission for Democracy, put an end to the vivid disputes triggered by the 'Status Law' and largely helped restoring the governmental cooperation between Hungary and Romania (Iordachi 2001). The good cooperation led to what was unconceivable only few years before, namely to common government sessions of joint Romanian and Hungarian governments, gathered in Hungary or in Romania in special meetings where to discuss common economic and political projects. The cooperation not only helped to ease ethnic tension in Transylvania, but to facilitate cooperation and mutual support for NATO and EU membership. One of the most vivid fears of Romanians, to have Hungary integrated into regional organizations and Romania being kept apart, was lifted with Romania's accession to NATO in 2004 and to the European Union in 2007, only few years after Hungary's accession in 1999 and 2004, respectively. The delay in accessing both NATO and EU memberships was due exclusively to technical reasons, on the one hand, and to the democratic deficit that was accumulated by Romania during the early phases of transition, on the other hand. Despite the high expectations of the Romanian politicians and public opinion, Romania was not prepared to get full NATO membership in 2004, as well as it was not yet ready to join the European Union in 2004. The democratic process was, however, unstoppable. Its inertia led to Romania's EU accession in company of another laggard, namely Bulgaria.

5.3 Romania's democratic trajectory: the successful laggard

With political and minority standards fulfilled, Romania focused on economic and institutional issues, looking to getting full NATO and EU membership. The delay recorded with respect to other former communist countries in Central and Eastern Europe, who joined earlier on NATO and the European Union, put high pressure on the Romanian government between 2000 and 2004. Although it was the same governing party as in the early stages of the democratic transition, PDSR (then relabeled PSD) managed to solve much of the pending problems that constitute solid barriers for European accession. This was especially the case of full marketization (Careja 2011) and the complete alignment to EU standards. The PSD government headed by Adrian Năstase pushed for mass privatization and property restitution, despite the initial party's reluctance for privatization and restitution (Mungiu-Pipiddi and Ştefan 2012). At the same time, PSD government completed the hard work of harmonizing the internal legislation with the EU standards, technically known as the 'Acquis communautaire'. In practice, this meant adopting and adapting the EU regulation standards to dozens of economic, social and administrative domains in Romania.

During the negotiation process with the European Commission, Romania was included in the second wave of accession, alongside Bulgaria. They completed the group of former communist states and their accession officially put an end to the post-communist transition. Romania and Bulgaria have been connected during the negotiation phase not only because they were the laggards, but also because their economic and political situations were much similar. From an economic perspective, Romania and Bulgaria started much later to accomplish reforms and have faced similar economic problems, reflected by regional statistics. From a historic perspective prior to communism, these largely agrarian countries were also regarded as less developed than other countries in the region (Roberts 1951), although the entire region was less developed than Western European countries (Chirot 1991). The table below summarizes the political and economic situation in 1999, just before the start of the negotiation process leading to full EU membership.

As presented in the Tab. 5.1, the economic and political indicators for the two countries were much similar. Although they were democracies in terms of civil and political rights, they were both affected by low direct investments, relatively high unemployment, rule of law deficit and significant levels of perceived corruption. Unsurprisingly, economic openness, direct investments and corruption are related issues. Corruption was, in fact, a major issue in both countries for decades, since informal payments, bribery and networks of informal relations replaced the functioning of a mature market economy, affecting numerous social and economic domains (Grigorescu 2006; Holmes 2009; Radin 2009). With the consolidation of market institutions and mass privatization, Romania and Bulgaria managed to reach the required standard for joining EU, which they did at January the 1st, 2007. They still are however subject to periodical investigation and control from the European Commission, especially until serious efforts will be made in both countries to tackle corruption (Hein 2015). This investigation is possible through a mechanism for cooperation and control, in place since 2007 and never lifted, despite the visible improvement of Romanian and Bulgarian standards for rule of law, transparency and effective fight against corruption.

Although they were labeled as laggards (Noutcheva and Bechev 2008), Romania and Bulgaria were finally more successful than other countries in the region. Despite the initial democratic gap when compared to new democracies in Central Europe, their European Union accession in 2007 confirmed

Tab. 5.1: Economic and political indicators for Romania and Bulgaria

	Romania	Bulgaria
GDP/capita – 1998 (USD)*	1697	1700
Foreign direct investments/capita 1990-1998 (USD)**	201	168
Unemployment – 1998 (%)*	10.3	12
Trade balance – 1998 (mil. USD)**	- 3521	- 702
Current account balance – 1998 (%GDP)*	- 7.9	- 2.3
FH rating of Political Rights – 1999***	2	2
FH rating of Civil Liberties – 1999***	3	2
FH – NiT Democratization score – 1999****	3	3
FH – NiT Rule of Law – 1999****	4	4
FH – NiT Economic Liberalization – 1999****	4	4
Corruption Perception Index – 1999*****	2.9	3.5

* BERD, *Transition Report Update*, April 1999; ** UN – Economic Commission for Europe, *Economic Survey of Europe*, 1999, no. 2; *** Freedom House, *Freedom in the World*, 2000; **** Freedom House, *Nations in Transit*, 2000; ***** Transparency International, 2000.

their complete democratic trajectory. Compared with Moldova or Ukraine, both Romania and Bulgaria avoided the uncertainty induced by the democratic regime instability specific to the former, with democratic efforts being followed by stagnation or even serious setbacks, an ongoing oscillation between East and West, democracy and authoritarianism (Dragoman 2015a; Munro 2007). Even the 2004 "Orange revolution" in Kyiv, despite representing an earthquake and setting the signal for other street rallies against other authoritarian regimes (Bunce and Wolchik 2006; Hale 2006), provoked mere public disappointment by the series of corruption scandals, presidential clientelism and the persistent oligarchy controlling the economy and mass media (Ryabinska 2011).

At the same time, both countries democratically evolved better than countries from the Western Balkans. Although they were not free of ethnic tensions, Romania and Bulgaria accepted the severe European conditionality and significantly improved minority rights. Romania even imposed higher standards in this domain, moving from laggard to leader (Ram 2009). This is much contrasting with the democratic trajectories of Serbia, Bosnia and even Croatia (Ramet and Matic 2007; Ramet, Hassenstab and Listhaug 2017), for example, where minority issues combined with the democratic deficit and further complicated the European accession process. When exiting from the former Yugoslavia, Serbia had great difficulties in accommodating minority issues with national-building and democratization, placing itself in a stage of incomplete democracy that combined elections with a large range of restrictions regarding effective opposition, civil and political rights (Ramet, Listhaug and Dulic 2011). This is much similar to the democratic deficit combined with nationhood issues in Moldova, where the management of minority issues turned complicated by the civil war that broke up the republic of Moldova and gave birth to a *de-facto* state in Trasnistria (Crowther 1998; Protsyk 2012; Tudoroiu 2011). From this perspective, Romania integrated the group of successful countries which overpassed the triple transition (Kuzio 2001) and joined the European Union, being similar to Baltic rather than to Balkan countries (Clemens 2010). Democracy in Romania is as stable as it was in the case of all other former communist countries which previously joined the European Union. As it will be noticed later on in this volume, Romanian democracy will prove even more solid when compared with serious setbacks to be recorded recently in Hungary and Poland, for example, countries which have been long time labeled as the democratic leaders of the Eastern European region.

6 Why no backsliding? Populism and the unrestricted use of executive power following the 2007 EU accession

The European conditionality proved to be the necessary condition for political elites to behave responsibly. In the essential relationship between citizens and elites, the virtuous circle described by Putnam (1993) was in fact fueled by the general commitment to attaining NATO and EU membership. The relationship described by Putnam is a direct one, linking critical yet satisfied citizens (one would say satisfied yet more and more critical citizens) to responsible and responsive elites. The input given by critical citizens is turned into valuable and effective public policies by those elites, who benefit of renewed support by more and more critical citizens, who switch the object of their request and support. Finally, the political system is strengthened by the perpetual interaction between active and engaged citizens, on one hand, and responsible elites, on the other hand. However, the quality of public policies oriented towards the general purpose of accessing NATO and the EU was much more the work of external conditionality, than the pure and conscientious willingness of the political elites, and much less the effect of citizens' pressure. The low impact of civic engagement on public elites' responsiveness, underlined in the first chapters of the volume, is to be unraveled by an essential change in the conditionality operating upon political elites.

All over Central and Eastern Europe, lifting external conditionality by NATO and EU membership made room for the expression of the unrestricted use of executive power. Focusing especially on changes occurring in Romania and Bulgaria, Ganev (2013) mapped several key issues in post-communist politics that are various types of corrupt activities, legislative and behavioral changes that undermined previously stable normative frameworks and, finally, a reversal of a general tendency towards the institutional stability known as "state building". Far from being a collection of disparate empirical findings, the new data configures a new strategy for linking post-accession changes in local elite behavior to the EU's (in)ability to keep on its conditionality that effectively worked during the pre-accession period. The new data enable Ganev (2013, 27) to propose a novel concept that could more accurately unravel the profound change in local elites' behavior. This is the concept of "post-accession hooliganism":

"might be used as a device for the systematization of disparate empirical data and thus enable us to order familiar analytical tropes and images – the corrupt official, the self-interested legislator, or the local leader who covets Brussels's approval – around a general theme: how the sticks and carrots of the EU affected the behavior of democratically elected elites in Eastern Europe".

The juxtaposition of the *pre*-accession and *post*-accession periods raises the question of the EU effective conditionality. Does it really induce to local elites to consciously embrace and internalize the set of normative principles of a peaceful, democratic, and prosperous Europe, asks Ganev, or it just motivates those elites temporarily and superficially to refrain their selfish impulses for overwhelming political domination and quick material gain? The answer is more evident when the whole region is taken into account, not only Romania and Bulgaria. Elites' willingness to control the political system and their subsequent shift from legitimate political changes to more personal attempts to bend rules in order to consolidate in power is by no means related to Romania and Bulgaria's democratic trajectories. As stressed out in the first part of the chapter, the democratic setback is one of the most intriguing political phenomena to be recorded in Central and Eastern Europe following the successful NATO and EU integration. It raises the question of the solidity of the overall democratization process, as well as it challenges the idea of sovereignty in those former communist countries that are now part of the European Union. The current conflicts between governing parties in Poland and Hungary and the European Commission stress the issue of the limits of the governing parties in shaping internal politics and policies. In this respect, the conservative revolutions in Central and Eastern Europe could be seen as either emancipation of local relevant political actors, renewing the pre-communist discourse about the nation and the specific national culture, or as a serious threat against democratic consolidation (Bozóki 2016). If the second answer is to be chosen, this perspective raises serious doubts about the degree of democratic consolidation attributed to successful country-cases and casts some shadows on the optimistic evaluation of the overall democratization process in the region.

6.1 Rising populism as 'post-accession hooliganism' in Central and Eastern Europe

As expressed by Ganev (2013), despite its theoretical imperfections, the concept of post-accession hooliganism has a considerable heuristic potential. As it is difficult to fully use it, since it was construed by the author as a Weberian ideal type, we empirically approximate one of its subtypes with illiberal populism, noticing 'hooligans' reluctance to comply with EU conditionality, namely the rule of law, constitutional stability and good governance (Rupnik 2007; Zielonka 2007). In fact, transition in Central and Eastern Europe was generally defined by a liberal consensus, especially with respect to the common objective of NATO and EU integration, namely the supremacy of the constitutional order and the effort for economic liberalization. From this perspective, external conditionality worked as a powerful anesthetic that inhibited unreliable, irresponsible and irresponsive political elites. Now, as the conditionality cannot really work anymore for most on the countries, excepting Romania and Bulgaria that are still partially under the EU's mechanism of post-integration control, consensus can be removed and internal politics be reshaped by resurgent post-accession hooliganism, with visible effects on democratic standards (Levitz and Pop-Eleches 2010). Post-accession hooligans refuse to obey to the separation of powers and to acknowledge the existence of politically neutral institutions, as courts of justice and especially constitutional courts, central banks, supervising and ruling institutions for mass media. They claim to speak for the real sovereign people and therefore despise all intermediate liberal democratic institutions that mediate representation (Bugaric 2008). They persistently claim for direct democracy and support charismatic leaders that channel social discontent against elites who oppose them and whom they depict as rigged against ordinary people (Krastev 2007; Jones 2007). Under their political action, democratic political regimes in the region witnessed the unrestricted use of executive power in the logic of the revival of political arbitrary, alongside partisanship and abuse, in areas where consensus was brutally brought down following the EU accession (Rupnik 2007). Their political action could further fuel the irrationalism and anti-intellectualism of the economically frustrated middle-class and finally help the resurgence of social conservatism and authoritarianism, as it is the current case in Hungary and Poland (Bozóki 2016; De Lange and Guerra 2009; Enyedi 2016; Pappas 2008; Varga 2008).

In fact, post-accession hooligans could be easily labeled as populists. Speaking for the people, fighting allegedly corrupt elites and willing to reshape the institutional framework in the benefit of the people, they reinforce authoritarian tendencies by claiming more power in order to put in practice their political agenda (Eke and Kuzio 2000). But populism is multifaceted. As emphasized by Schmitter (2007), there are both vices and virtues of populism. On the one hand, populists dissolve partisan loyalties and rational choices among various political programmes, without replacing them with something of their own; they recruit uniformed persons with no clear political preferences and who look for emotional rather than programmatic political satisfactions; they make promises and raise expectations that generally cannot be fulfilled; they identify aliens and alien powers as scapegoats for their own political failures and, most important, may undermine democracy by the support provided by the army or security forces, which make their democratic removal from office unlikely. On the other hand, populist politicians and parties help reshape sclerotic party loyalties and dissolve party coalitions that are based on secret agreements, and they recruit and mobilize previously apathetic persons. By focusing on disparate and hidden political issues, they help articulate previously neglected cleavages and demands; they replace political immobilism and widen the range of possible political solutions to collective problems. All in all, when electorally defeated, populism leaves behind a reinvigorated party system. From this perspective, populism is more like a symptom of democracy, rather than a defect of democracy (De Waele and Pacześniak 2010).

In both Western and Eastern Europe, populists claim for direct democracy, appeal to the 'pure people' and support charismatic leaders who channel social discontent against the 'corrupt elite', conceived as rigged against ordinary people in an attempt to deprive the sovereign people of their rights, values, prosperity, identity and voice (Albertazzi and McDonnell 2007; Jones 2007; Mudde 2004). They fuel the irrationalism and anti-intellectualism of the economically frustrated middle-class and support the resurgence of social conservatism and authoritarianism. The difference between West and East is the capacity of containing such radical populist movements in the framework of the liberal democratic system. Whereas Western democracies put those parties perceived as populist on the fringe of the political system and managed to keep them out of executive power (Mudde 2007), in Central and Eastern Europe populist parties put in place favorable mechanisms for consolidating in power, silence critics, destructurate democratic institutions and undermine opposition parties.

In Romania, we identify post-accession hooligans by their populist characteristics, and first of all by their propensity of speaking for the people. The very mechanism of speaking for the people raises the moral question of how populists imagine people and how much people value for populists themselves. Since populists use emotional, simplistic and manipulative discourses directed at the 'gut feelings' of the people, or put in place opportunistic policies aimed at 'buying' the support of the people (Krastev 2007), the question seems pertinent. Moreover, as we unravel here by the Romanian case-study, persistently claiming to speak for the people may turn into what Sartori (1987) would label a 'demolatry', a permanent discussion about the people with no real attention paid to the people, and finally, a total despise for the real people. The changing attitude towards people, who turns from a very source of legitimacy into a bitter political enemy, lies at the heart of populist politics in Romania between 2007 and 2014.

6.2 Speaking for the people: 'they stand by them, we stand by you!'

In Romania, as in other countries in the region, populists gained power by exploiting people's legitimate expectations for political change, fairness, transparency, and accountability. The difficult negotiations for joining the European Union only helped to expose Romania's multiple weaknesses, which populists used in the 2004 presidential election campaign. By promising a bitter fight against endemic corruption and state institutions' inefficiency, Traian Băsescu and his party, the populist Democrat Party (which was relabeled in 2007 as Democrat Liberal Party, Partidul Democrat Liberal – PDL), won the 2004 elections under the banner of state reinvigoration, modernization and constitutional reform. This electoral victory marks the beginning of an alliance between populists and the people which is very clearly stated by next general electoral campaign slogan in 2008, 'they stand by them, we stand by you!'. Whereas 'they' refers to the corrupt elite, 'we' epitomizes populists and 'you' the supporting people.

One cannot understand this campaign slogan without proper references to populists' fight against political elites between 2004 and 2008. Often accused of pervasive corruption, the power elites are fought by populists as they are seen as inheriting their influence from the previous power networks of the communist regime and are accused of effectively ruling with the support of the judiciary system and of a large part of mass media, which they actually own. By labeling parliament as the expression of the most corrupt and obsolete power elite, the courts of justice as the very expression of a privileged and disrespectful interest group and the free media as a pressure instrument used to manipulate the 'people', Romanian populists strongly emphasized these issues during their 2008 successful campaign.

The violent attacks against parliament, pinpointed by populists as the ultimate expression of irresponsiveness and abuse, originate in the 2007 political split between classical and moderate liberals from the PNL and the PDL. Although back in 2004 they have joint forces and thus succeeded to defeat the ruling Social-Democrat Party in both parliamentary and presidential elections, essential differences between the PNL prime minister Călin Popescu-Tăriceanu and the Romanian president Traian Băsescu led to an unsolved conflict that culminated with the impeachment of the president Băsescu in 2007 by a newly constituted PNL-PSD majority in parliament. Although the president was put back in office by the will of the majority of citizens expressed by the dismissal refer- endum, his relationship with the parliament will never be the same. In fact, 2007 and the failed referendum for impeaching the president is the defining moment of victorious populism.

Inspired by people's commitment, Băsescu promised to use *ad hoc* popular consultations every three months, by gathering in University square ("Piața Universității") in Bucharest in the last Sunday of the month. There the voice of the people should be followed by the populist president, who should adapt its political views and actions accordingly. "Piața Universității" is an iconic place in newly democratic Romania, since it harbored the anti-communist mass rallies of the opposition parties back in early 1990. Since then, "Piața Universității" is a symbol for the struggle towards democratization, and the place where the oppo- sition parties celebrated their 1996 electoral victory against PDSR. Băsescu's promise for *ad hoc* popular consultations was done following another promise, one he never kept. In April 2007, when the parliament was preparing to impeach him, Traian Băsescu declared that instead of waiting for a dismissal referendum, he would rather step down, quit his office and run again in new presidential elections. In Băsescu's terms, this move would take him less than five minutes! Following the impeachment, he never stepped down and, later on, considered this possible move as a plot of his political enemies.

The failed impeachment consolidated populists' claims of fighting cor- rupt power elites and consolidated the image of the president as a victorious hero. Following the impeachment, populists claimed that parliament's allegedly privileged position has to be challenged through a new institutional design. Launching his counteroffensive by pitting his personal popularity against the low esteem for parliament (Marian and King 2010), and according to his consti- tutional right to appoint referendums, the restored president called for a serious change in the composition of the parliament. A referendum was therefore settled out to accompany regular presidential elections in 2009. The wording of the ref- erendum included populists' proposal of reducing the number of MPs from 471 to no more than 300, and the passage to a mono-cameral representative body, replacing the current bi-cameral assembly. The majority of the electors (50.16%) voted in favor of the referendum, accompanying a narrow majority of voters who confirmed Traian Băsescu back in office.

The connection between Romanian populists and the people they allegedly fight for is also visible in the strong professionalization of electoral campaigning. Popular music, for instance, was acknowledged for its communication poten- tial and seriously taken into account by populists as valuable electoral vehicle in order to mobilize generally undereducated and disengaged young people. As those young people form a political target generally difficult to reach by ordinary means, as emphasized below, populists ingeniously used a very popular music genre in Romania, called 'manele' (Dragoman et al. 2012). Thus the privileged relationship between the populist leader and the people, in the early stages, is to be also found in popular music.

As an essential social product, popular music offers compelling insights into the social world we live in. Popular music is a social sign because it creates an effect in the perceiver that is not only aesthetic, but socially meaningful. Moreover, popular music is a sign because it appeals to the emotions of a generation, particularly a young generation (Matusitz 2010). Thus popular music carries out cultural images and symbols that surround the music and generate a particular narrative (Stratton 1989). Popular music may also serve as vehicle for frustration, anger and protest against established values and norms (Adorno 1980), since music is probably the most suitable way for young people to express not only their identity (Griffin 2011), but their political knowledge and orientations, in indirect or more direct manners (Baker 2010; Leung and Kier 2008). In our peculiar case, the popular music is epitomized by 'manele' (singular: 'manea'), a series of widely popular songs in Romania that are considered to accurately express citizens' social and political knowledge and orientations. Those songs are widespread cultural items, especially among young people, since the beginning of the post-communist transition in 1990. It is not unusual to hear 'manele' in buses or in railway stations, in taxis or in restaurants.

The general perspective emphasized by 'manele' is gloomy, as it depicts remote social forces that tend to overwhelm marginal individuals. Whose forces are conceived as an impersonal social environment largely defined by hatred, a general environment labeled as a 'mean world', where no one can be trusted and where marginal single individuals feel powerless. Whereas visible enemies work as a booster for social competition, with individuals strongly motivated to overpass and defeat their covetous enemies, the 'mean world' is full of uncertainty. In this gloomy world, even close friends and allies may turn into bitter enemies, where the constant suspicion about close friends who attempt to coax, seduce and dupe. Covetous, ungrateful and misleading friends thus add new significance to the 'mean world', helping to intensify the powerless and hopeless feeling. This is exactly the political environment exploited by populists in order to predicate the difference between the populist hero and its alleged enemies.

It is to be noticed that, on the other hand, 'manele' largely express a process of differentiation of the hero, the one who finally defeats its enemies and manages to overpass life's difficulties. In the predication process, manele's singer, who embodies the hero, generally portrays himself as 'cooler', cleverer, richer, more hard working. The difference is predicated by comparing manale's hero to its social rivals, who generally envy him for his social success. By translating this social pattern of rivalry into the political field, populists forged the image of the populist leader, the presidential candidate and finally the president Băsescu, who finally manages to overcome its political enemies and keeps fighting them once back in office, despite their attempt to impeach him. This image was constructed and spread out by the means of various vehicles, including 'manele'. A special 'manea' (singular from 'manele', let us emphasize again), called "Maneaua lui Băsescu. Să trăiți bine!" ("Băsescu's manea. Long live well!"), was written for the 2008-2009 presidential and parliamentary election campaigns, where the incumbent president Băsescu is portrayed as the true 'people's' hero. The subtitle of the 'manea' reproduces exactly the slogan used earlier in the 2004 campaign by then the challenger candidate Băsescu, which was 'Long live well!'. Later on, the president Băsescu declared that it was definitely a wish (as people make at birthdays or holidays) and not a true promise. Only the people have to be blamed if they have taken it for a serious campaign promise.

The assertion of his solid popularity is based in the 'manea' on the first name of the president, which is Traian, emphasized in the 'manea' text as a Latin name, echoing that of the Roman Emperor Trajan, who is considered one of the earliest national heroes due to its historical contribution to the genesis of the Romanian people. As emphasized by the Romanian national anthem, dating from the 1848 Revolution, the emperor's name relates to the Roman conquest in the second century AD of the lands inhabited today by the Romanian people.

In connection with the gloomy social world put forward by this popular music genre, the populist hero is forced to experience once again the drama generally depicted by the 'manele'. He is betrayed by his closest ally, namely by the prime minister Tăriceanu, a rogue and ungrateful (former) 'brother' that has been seduced with large sums of money by president's worse enemies. Those enemies are, in fact, peculiar to Romanian populist discourse, and they are number of interest groups. Since interest groups that allegedly attempt to control Romania are common place in the populists' discourse, it is not surprising to find them pointed out in the 'manele' texts as president Băsescu's bitter enemies. They have thus plotted against him and unfairly attacked him from behind, while impeaching him in 2007.

The special 'manea' composed for accompanying PDL and president Băsescu's electoral campaigns in 2008-2009, is to be taken as the climax of populism, when the people was supporting the populist hero in its bitter fight against people's enemies, regrouped under the large banner of interest groups rigged against ordinary people. In fact, 'manele' strongly underline a dimension that is inherent to populists' discourse, namely the ultimate struggle against a terrible enemy. In their reductionist view, the institutional conflict from 2007 between democratic institutions, the parliament and the government, on the one hand, and the president, on the other hand, turned out to be a savage conflict for political survival. This is, in the end, how PDL's slogan from 2008 is to be understood, as the logic of the bitter conflict between 'us' and 'them' that spreads across the whole society, opposing the populists and them, the opposition parties in toxic alliance with a large array of interest groups, power elites and people's enemies. The accession to power of populists marks a special landmark in Romanian politics. Their political action directed towards the consolidation in power with all costs and their subsequent hostile attitude towards the people that supported them only months before is another characteristic of the populist rule.

6.3 Populists in power: institutional change and political control

Unlike the Western cases, where populism is merely a political phenomenon limited to an electoral expression, populism in power is a new feature that raises new theoretical questions and offers new perspectives. In fact, in Western settings, populism is a long lasting phenomenon, a pathological normalcy (Mudde 2010) merely related to anti-immigration issues, in combination with social frustration and economic deprivation (Akkerman 2012; Kriesi 2014; Taggart 1995). More recently, populism successfully combines with Euroscepticism (Arzheimer 2015; Clarke et al. 2016), by triggering the mass reaction of the British electorate voting for UK leaving the European Union, or with regionalism, by fueling the electoral success of parties like the *Lega Nord* in Italy (Albertazzi and McDonnell 2010). Despite some brief episodes when right-wing populist parties have formed governing coalition, their presence in government was much criticized by the public opinion, generally preventing them to re-enter coalitions following the end of the mandate. This is largely different from the Eastern European cases, where populists win elections, form various government coalitions or even govern alone, consolidating in power and seeking to win the subsequent elections from their governmental positions. This is the case in Romania, where PDL consolidated in power and turned from the initial willingness to reinvigorate state and reshape politics to numerous strategies to maintain power with all costs, including despising the public opinion and the will of the people, as expressed by referenda.

It goes without saying that populism is not a recent feature in Romanian politics. Since the early 1990s, when the first changes within the political system took place, populists tried to combine the Romanian nationalism used by the communist regime in its latter period (Chen 2003; Verdery 1995) with the popular fears raised by sharp social change and economic uncertainty. The combination gave birth to a populist party that was the populist actor of the political space for almost two decades, namely Greater Romania Party (Partidul România Mare – PRM) (Pop-Eleches 2001). Its slow but constant decline opened the door to other populist parties, including Dan Diaconescu People's Party (Partidul Poporului Dan Diaconescu – PPDD) and the PDL itself. The difference between PDL and other populist parties is its access to power, its willingness to shape policies and politics according to its populist discourse. This is why PDL is taken here as a case study for post-accession hooliganism and for ruling populism. In order to give a full perspective on the political trajectory of successful and declining populism, we will focus on PDL's strategy of maintaining in power as much as possible and its ability of conserving electoral support even in times of political defeat, as it was the case in 2012.

6.3.1 Populist consolidation in power: looking for a favorable electoral system

Once in office in 2004, the president Traian Băsescu and the Democrat-Liberal Party seemed trying answering to legitimate claims for political system reinvigoration, fairness, transparency and accountability. Using a personal political style labeled as 'triage democracy' (King and Sum 2011), in fact a strategy of triggering and solving successive political crises in order to master the public agenda, the president put in line truth and justice slogans, promising the access to the former communist political police files and to morally clean the Romanian society (Stan 2002), with proposals for the substantial revisions of the electoral law, changing the legislative-executive balance of power and the size and structure of the legislature. In line with the limited verbal condemnation of communism (Dragoman 2014), those initial proposals looked more like proposals for increasing institutional efficiency. On a closer examination in the context of populism consolidating in power, it soon became visible that the actions taken by populists were directed against the parliament and against all political bodies that intermediate representation.

For almost two decades following the 1989 revolution, the MPs in Romania were elected by using a proportional representation (PR) formula. Despite the benefits of proportionality for minority parties during the initial phase of democratization (Mihailescu 2008), PR came under severe criticism due to its mechanism of candidate selection. The decision of parties in selecting candidates was designated by many intellectuals and politicians as a significant obstacle in reinvigorating political parties' offer. Focusing on candidate selection mechanisms, which were not always free of corruption and served many times to appoint inefficient politicians, many NGOs and the public opinion largely entrusted electoral reform and the passage from PR to a single-member district majoritarian system (SMD) as a clear mean of enhancing transparency and responsibility, fostering electoral competition, and compelling improvements in the quality of representative government (Marian and King 2010).

The opportunity was largely used by populists to fight against parliament as the ultimate expression of the corrupt elite, retrenched in parliament and willing to ignore people's desire for transparency and efficiency. Under pressure, PNL in government at the time, issued a legislative proposal based on the German mixed-member model that carefully balances legitimacy through district-based elected MPs with overall proportional fair political representation, and this proposal was adopted by the parliament. In conflict with the PNL prime minister, the president Băsescu contested the law before the Constitutional court and succeeded to invalidate it in November 2007. His preference, in accordance with PDL, was the first-past-the-post system (FPTP), and his only second option was a French type majoritarian two-round runoff system (TR). Using his constitutional right to appoint national referenda, he decided to accompany the election of Romania's European deputies in November 2007 by a popular referendum on the topic of the uninominal voting system. Only the low turnout disabled president's proposal to be validated, despite four-fifths of the electors voting 'yes'.

The conflict between the president, who was speaking for the people, and the parliamentary majority lead by PNL ended in a compromise, that is a complicated single-member district uninominal voting system (SMD), which turned the electoral system from a very difficult to understand and complicated to operate system to a more convoluted and obscure one, a step forward in order to achieve district-based representation, but with no effects on the selection of candidates and on the 'purifying' of the political class (Marian and King 2010). Moreover, PDL used the new electoral provisions in 2008 not as to support the district-based representation, but to win as many parliamentary seats and consolidate in power. Instead of candidate-centered campaign, PDL members used a nation-wide, unified, giant electoral campaign supported by the president's popularity. They did not increase the legitimacy of the elected representatives by appointing candidates that lived and worked in local districts or county constituencies or who felt eager to establish connections with the local contexts and electors. In 2012, many top PDL leaders who were MPs incumbent candidates left their initial constituencies and moved into PDL's strongholds, looking for a safe vote (Gherghina 2013; Giugăl et al. 2017). Back in 2008, following the successful elections, they did not help consolidate the much awaited new linkage between electors and MPs, as they encouraged MPs from other parties in parliament to despise their responsibility towards districts of origin, to break with their initial party ranks and join PDL in order to secure a 'fabricated' majority. All in all, they did little in helping the parliament and the MPs to gain in public prestige and support and worked against the consolidation of the representative institutions, since only populists were entitled to speak for the people.

For the years to come following the 2007 referendum on the topic of the uninominal voting system, populists used the referendum's outcome in order to pinpoint parliament as an obsolete and vicious institution, refusing to put in place people's will. Since the referendum was not compulsory, even the PDL majority in parliament was not eager to adopt a roughly majoritarian electoral system, keeping in mind that such a system could become a future supplementary obstacle, adding to the fading popular support. In fact, populists' preference for the FPTP system was purely instrumental. Following the no confidence vote in parliament and the dismissal of the PDL government in 2012, the new majority in parliament formed by PNL and PSD managed to pass a new electoral law for the subsequent parliamentary elections scheduled for the fall 2012, essentially based on pure majoritarian, namely on the FPTP system. Facing a severe electoral defeat, PDL contested the law to the Constitutional court and the court overruled the low, keeping in place the electoral provisions from 2008. It became obvious afterwards that overruling the FPTP system was the only chance for PDL to keep its parliamentary representation, following its disastrous electoral defeat in the 2012 elections. Before discussing about populists' electoral defeat from 2012, let us focus on their efforts of controlling the political system and undermining opposition's political resources.

6.3.2 Weakening the legislature: reducing both MPs' number and credibility

After the successful electoral campaign in 2008, using the new electoral provisions, populists overtly turned against parliament. The president used once again of his constitutional right to appoint referenda and called the people to get rid of the sclerotic political class embodied by the parliament. The wording of the referendum was president's proposal of reducing the number of MPs from 471 to no more than 300, and passing from a bicameral to a mono-cameral representative body. Symbolically, the referendum was set to accompany president's own re-election for a second term, in November 2009. A slim majority of the electors

(50.16 %) voted in favor of the referendum. Since in Romania only the constitutional referenda are compulsory and since the 2009 referendum was consultative and not legally binding, it was the parliament to decide upon the change. Its reluctance to adopt a law designed to reduce its members was once again the perfect argument used by populists in their struggle against the allegedly obsolete, corrupt and abusive institution of the parliament.

How could one explain populists' success in stirring and turning people against parliament? The explanation could be twofold. On the one hand, as mentioned earlier, populists pitted their popularity, and especially that of the president Băsescu, against the low esteem for parliament (Marian and King 2010). As in other countries in the region during transition, parliament benefited of very low levels of institutional trust (Lühiste 2006). During transition, the Romanian parliament was largely perceived as a collective body that merely responds to citizens' needs, but was very effective in defending the legal impunity of the MPs who were under prosecutors' investigation. This already bad image only helped populists to depict parliament as futile and ineffective, as the ultimate expression of irresponsiveness and abuse. In fact, trust in parliament is dependent on the way citizens conceive the accountability and the reliability of the political system, meaning that trust in parliament is higher in countries with low levels of corruption, proportional representation and long time, consolidated functional democracy, and lower in former communist countries (Van Der Meer 2001).

On the other hand, populists balanced the alleged parliament's ineffectiveness with the executive power prestige and claimed efficacy. The symbolic conflict turned into effective confrontation in 2007, when the parliament impeached and suspended president Băsescu, only to see him back in office following a substantial vote in the required national referendum for impeachment (Gherghina and Miscoiu 2013). The restoration of the president in office only boosted populists' claims to weaken the parliament. They proposed that a failed attempt of impeachment should automatically trigger the dissolution of parliament. In president's words, "if the referendum confirms the president, then the Parliament is dissolved". In fact, the president's prerogative to dissolve the parliament was especially denied by the Constitution in 1991, which makes an effort to create a president powerful enough, but not too powerful to change the parliamentary features of the Romanian political system, despite the popular election of the president. In theory, the president should work as 'mediator' between state institutions, which really makes him a president from a typical parliamentary system. The menaces of the president to dissolve the parliament, similar to those he made during the presidential campaign in 2009, are out of the scope of the presidential power set up by the Romanian constitution.

The second impeachment of the president Băsescu in June 2012 marks the climax of the populist attacks against parliament. When asked by the parliament about the constitutional opportunity of the second impeachment, the Constitutional court clearly acknowledged and stated president's lack of neutrality and sanctioned his decision to abandon his mediator status. In fact, Traian Băsescu abandoned since 2005 his mediator status and acted much more like a *de facto* party leader, negotiating with parties for securing a safe majority into parliament for PDL, openly attacking opposition parties and hostile mass media and overtly supporting his favorite candidate for the presidency of PDL, his former party. His practice of frequently heading PDL meetings was even acknowledged as 'customary' by PDL leaders. Moreover, the menaces to dissolve the parliament in November 2009 were also made in order to put pressure on the parliamentary parties, if his favorite candidate for prime minister would not have been supported by the parliament. Finally, the PDL president Emil Boc was appointed prime minister in December 2009. Between 2009 and 2012, populists have secured the overwhelming power, by cumulating the parliamentary majority, the two executive branches of the executive power, namely the government and the president, and by appointing new judges to the Constitutional court. Additionally, the PDL government replaced hundreds of civil servants with obedient and helpful new public servants in central and local administration, while the PDL majority in parliament replaced the directors of the public television and of the National Audio-Visual Council, the body regulating radio and TV media. Only the sharp erosion of their popularity, due to severe cuts in social benefits during the severe economic crisis and the unprecedented corruption scandals affecting high government officials, including tourism, economy, communication, education and sport ministers in the PDL government, made the prime minister Emil Boc to be the first prime minister dismissed by the parliament since 1989. Although we have no room here to discuss about this issue and prefer to discuss it in the next chapter, let us briefly emphasize that many top PDL leaders who were ministers in the Boc government have been arrested in 2015, charged with accusations of fraud, abuse and corruption. Abuses were mainly done when dealing with public owned companies and public institutions in the energy, communication and education sectors, as well as with property restitution agencies. The former PDL minister of sports, Monica Iacob-Ritzi, has been sentenced to five years in prison for fraud and corruption. She has been involved in the illegal financing of the 2009 European election campaign.

The impeachment from June 2012 was taken by populists as a coup. Soon after the favorable vote in parliament, when the president Băsescu was suspended and the people asked to decide upon dismissal on a national referendum, as they already did in 2007, foreign embassies and the European Commission have been alerted in relation to a coup perpetrated in Romania, where the parliament has illegally suspended the president and deprived him of his legitimate power. The alert has been received with much concern and dissatisfaction by the German chancellery and personally by the presidents of the European Commission and of the European Parliament, but also by numerous members of the European People's Party, PDL's political family in the European Parliament. The confusion was such that many foreign embassies and European central institutions did not consult the Romanian constitution, where the impeachment procedure is legally stated, and accepted to support populists in Romania in their claims regarding the alleged coup that severely violated the democratic rules.

The impeachment procedure ended with a very controversial vote at the end of June 2012. Despite the huge share of electors voting 'yes' (7,4 million electors, meaning 88.7%, compared with the 5,2 million votes in favor of Băsescu in the second run-off ballot in 2009) the referendum was invalidated by the Constitutional court for technical reasons. The issue at stake was the required threshold for validation. Noticing the damage potential of the impeachment referenda, following the 2007 failed impeachment, the PDL majority in parliament amended in May 2011 the referendum law and set up a legal threshold. In order to validate a referendum, the participation should be at least 50 % plus one vote from the overall electorate. Defining the electorate was, in fact, the key for the legal invalidation of the referendum. Although a population census was done in 2011, unraveling a severe loss of population and an important external migration process, the PDL government did not make public its results. Therefore, the demographic benchmark used in 2012 was the available 2002 census, accompanied by unreliable and contradictory personal data issued by the Electoral Authority and the Interior Ministry. With significant differences between the figures put forward by various state authorities, the Constitutional court decided to invalidate the referendum. When the census data was finally made public in 2013, it turned out that the legal threshold imposed by populists as a technical safeguard was in fact surpassed in June 2012.

But the vote was also controversial for another reason. A successful impeachment would have prematurely ended the president's second term in office, a situation hard to conceive by the populists who still controlled the presidential power, but lost the parliamentary majority and their government was dismissed by the parliament in April 2012. The political struggle was focusing on the impeachment outcome, but the conflict was developing in a different political environment. Speaking for the people, in 2007 the president turned the failed impeachment in a boost for his fight against the corrupt and abusive political elite retrenched in parliament. In 2012, a successful impeachment would have confirmed the paradox of unpopular populists, adding the presidential impeachment to the dismissal of the PDL government. Therefore, a parallel strategy was to declare that voting to the referendum was undemocratic. The president himself made a televised statement and called for a democratic boycott as a mean for preserving the democracy. Moreover, the prosecutor Daniel Morar, head of the Anti-Corruption National Agency, stated in a televised address that 2 of the 8 million casted ballots were illegal, confirming that the boycott expressed by the president and his allies from PDL was justified. Despite the hundreds of citizens put under judicial investigation by the prosecutors the days following the referendum for alleged electoral fraud, few cases were sent by the prosecutors in court and merely a couple of people have been found guilty for minor electoral misconduct. If there were some electoral frauds, which is not surprising, the meager final judicial outcome is far from the alleged millions of illegally casted ballots. The move made by the populist propaganda is however much telling about the political strategy used by PDL to remain in power, despite the parliamentary dismantling of its political coalition formed with UDMR.

6.3.3 Populism and the dominance of the executive power

The 'presidentialisation' of the political system, as attempted by the populists, might undermine not only the legislative-executive balance of power and the consolidation of parliamentarism (Clark and Wittrock 2005), but even the quality of democracy (Linz 1990). Whereas they did not succeed in changing the overall constitutional framework as they initially intended by strengthening the presidential executive power, populists used extensively the existing constitutional provisions in order to impose the dominance of the executive power of the prime minister. This is not to say that PDL was the only party in power to push the legal provisions, but to stress that populists used a combined strategy to weaken and subordinate the parliament.

The primary observation is that populists used an existing tendency towards stronger majoritarian rule in order to consolidate in power, and only secondly set up clearly oriented strategies to undermine the parliament. The new Romanian constitution from 1991, following months of ardent debates, intended to offer to the Romanian post-communist society a new democratic framework that engulfed the logic of negotiation and compromise in an extremely conflictual political environment (Carey 2004). In fact, the early Romanian democratic political system reflects a rather consensual than majoritarian logic, when the system is analyzed according to the separation and the concentration of powers on the executive and federal dimensions (Lijphart 1984). It is true, the Romanian parliamentary system makes an effort to create a president powerful enough, but not too powerful to change its parliamentary features, despite the popular election of the president. The attempts made by populists to consolidate in power were in line with the transformations of the whole political system they wanted, especially with a concentration of power which is specific to majoritarian political systems. The prerogative of the president to dissolve the assembly, his right to dismiss the prime minister, they all point towards an attempt to consolidate the executive power.

It works the same for populists' willingness to get rid of the proportional representation and their quest for electoral systems that more easily 'manufacture' parliamentary majorities and strengthen the government branch. In specific settings, majoritarian electoral systems could undermine political competition (Fauvelle-Aymar and Lewis-Beck 2008), which may be a serious concern for unconsolidated democracies. The two-round runoff system (TR) favored by PDL in case that FPTP was not to be accepted, proves to be a destabilizing factor that inhibits democratic development, works to fragment the party-system and encourages the use of non-electoral means of exercising power (Birch 2007). On the one hand, political competition is based no more on the capacity of parties to select appropriate candidates as it partially was the case for PR, but on their capacity to use on their own profit the willingness of already popular personalities, often from the show-business area, to involve in a political competition and get elected. This new political competition mechanism could strongly affect the consolidation of still inchoate political parties. On the other hand, TR and even more obviously the FPTF would encourage electoral fraud, since the total amount of votes necessary to decide the winner is narrower than it ever was in TR and especially in PR. As underlined by Birch (2007), the electoral manipulation and misconduct in single-member districts under plurality and majority rule in Eastern Europe is significantly correlated with the proportion of seats elected under such electoral systems. FPTP and TR are far more advanced in shaping incentives to engage in electoral misconduct and severe violations of electoral integrity.

The adoption of a new electoral system was set to consolidate the executive, since populists were dissatisfied with the stability of the governing coalitions. This complaint was much in contrast with the effective stability of the Romanian governments. Unlike some parliamentary democracies that are characterized by short-lived executives, high party-system polarization and severe parliamentary instability, as the French Fourth Republic, Romania witnessed a rather stable executive, since only one government failed to get a confidence vote in 25 years of parliamentary democracy. When one takes into account all duly-constituted governments in Romania, he finds that Romanian government enjoyed a mean of 489 days in office (Conrad and Golder 2010). Although this time span is shorter than the overall mean of eleven Central Eastern European democracies between 1990 and 2008, it is significantly longer than it is in Poland or Latvia, and much longer than it was in the mentioned French Fourth Republic (9 months) or even in Finland (13 months) during the 1945–1980 period (Lijphart 1984). Moreover, the crisis percentage index calculated by Conrad and Golder (2010) as the percentage of time spent without duly-mandated governments is only 2.5 for Romania, which represents half of the overall mean of 5.2 for all eleven East European countries taken into account.

When all the institutional attempts to consolidate the executive power by amending the constitution or by changing the electoral law failed, populists turned against parliament by adopting new strategies. The first strategy was to literally flood the parliament's agenda with government emergency ordinances. Although emergency ordinances are acknowledged by the Constitution as legitimate means of the executive power for responding to urgent issues (catastrophes, natural disasters, large-scale accidents), populists in government turned the exception into a rule and issued a great number of such decrees that seriously inflated the parliamentary activity. Despite the fact that the emergency ordinances are to be finally voted by the parliament, they are effective from the moment when they are issued by the government. In practice, their consequences can hardly be erased by subsequent contrary decisions of the parliament. Moreover, those emergency ordinances, once issued, turn into a priority on parliament's agenda. As emphasized by the Freedom House report for 2012, the issuing of an inordinately high number of emergency ordinances was a severe government abuse of power. PDL government also abused of its right to issue such ordinances during the previous period, when it issued no more than 86 emergency ordinances in the first 6 months of 2009 for example, in cases when government's emergency intervention was not needed (Ştefan, Tapalagă and Ioniţă 2010). The matters concerned by those ordinances are rarely an emergency, as they generally pertain to public spending, acquisitions and commercial agreements unrelated to emergency situations as severe natural disasters or large scale catastrophes or accidents. Many of those ordinances, especially those aiming to regulate public acquisitions and commercial agreements, are now under judicial investigation. The prosecutors believe that they were merely related to electoral campaign strategies and not to emergency situations. We will emphasize the outcome of governmental corruption in the next chapter.

The second strategy used by PDL government is to shortcut the parliamentary debates and decisions and to replace them with executive responsibility endorsements. The domination model, described by this strategy, points toward the limitation and suppression of the legitimate contestation in parliament and abroad, in the public space. In fact, the endorsement procedure enables the government to automatically turn any of its proposals into effective law if the opposition in parliament does not demand for a confidence vote or if such vote is rejected by the majority in parliament. On the contrary, a confidence vote that fails automatically leads to the rejection of the proposal and to the dismissal of the government. Although this is a constitutional procedure, as it is clearly stated by the current constitution, it should remain an exceptional procedure. It can be used by a government in order to test the strength of its governing coalition or to make effective his political points of view, but it cannot be used as a normal legislative procedure. Despite the strong majority in parliament, PDL government headed by Emil Boc used 13 times on a row this procedure in order to turn proposals into effective laws. Although this is not at all illegal, this propensity for automatic law enacting only adds to the features of post-accession hooliganism, which despises the real people and makes substantial efforts to avoid free and democratic debate in parliament. This is a very serious democratic issue, noticing that the PDL government turned his proposals into effective laws in very sensitive and key areas, such as education, health care, public administration, budgetary and fiscal domains.

With the strengthening of the executive power, PDL displayed a low esteem for parliament and even for his own MPs. The treatment against his MPs during the required confidence vote demanded by the opposition following a governmental endorsement procedure is much telling. In order to avoid unpleasant situations that sometimes occurred during the confidence vote, while a very limited number of MPs overtly voted against their government, beginning with 2010, PDL MPs were not allowed by their party leaders to stand up, express their views or even vote in parliament. They were forced to be sited and wait for the end of the plenary session, with only the opposition MPs expressing their views and voting. Even it could be taken for a rigid party discipline measure, this is an undemocratic feature, limiting MPs freedom of speech and action and despising their representative mandates.

The third strategy used by the populists was to limit the sovereignty of the parliament by limiting the scope of his legislative capacity. Anticipating a future government failure in securing a parliamentary majority and the dismissal of the PDL government, the PDL majority passed in 2010 a law empowering the Constitutional court to judge on matters that previously exceeded the court's competence. Back in 1991, the Constitutional court was set up by the Constitution to impartially put in place the judicial review of constitutionality in the framework of a centralized system of judicial review, as other countries in the region did in the context on the uncertainty associated with competitive elections after 1989 (Moraski 2013). Although the Constitutional court was always asked to decide on any legal matter related to human and civil rights, the separation of powers and possible constitutional conflicts between institutions, the court was never able to decide on parliament's decisions which regarded other issues than those mentioned above. In other words, the parliament was the one to decide on political issues, as he currently embodies the national sovereignty. According to the new law (Law no. 177 from 2010, section 27), the Constitutional court has to decide on any matter, any time the court is notified, including the constitutionality of parliament's decisions and internal procedures and regulations. When the parliament tried indeed in 2012 to recover its full powers by the mean of a new law restricting courts' prerogatives to the extent of power the court enjoyed before 2010, the Court simply overruled the law and kept its ability to decide on political matters. The move made by the PDL majority in 2010 proved successful in 2012, when the Constitutional court rejected the new electoral law based on the FPTP system, giving PDL the unexpected opportunity to keep its parliamentary status and secure a few seats for his prominent leaders. Otherwise, PDL would have been totally defeated in the 2012 general elections, when no PDL candidate won the absolute majority of votes in the electoral constituency where they run, but benefited of the proportional provisions of the former electoral law from 2008 and thus secured his seat by the means of the overall redistribution of votes at national level. The ability of the populist party to avoid total electoral defeat by means of institutional arrangements is in line with its willingness to change the institutional design in order to consolidate in power. But this willingness sometimes exceeded the democratic limits, as it was the case with the attempt of limiting the opposition's political resources by postponing local elections scheduled for the spring 2012.

6.3.4 Preempting electoral defeat: postponing local elections

Whereas subordinating the legislative body to the executive branch, changing the electoral system for partisan purposes and appointing favorable judges to the Constitutional Court are clear measures directed towards power consolidation that remain at the limit of the democratic realm, postponing elections are by and large out of the democratic realm. As emphasized by Downs (1957), the rationality specific to the democratic system is maintained as long as the outcomes of any governmental action are not directed against the opposition's political resources. It means that the government is free to take any action would probably lead to its re-election, including all the economic measures imagined as necessary, ranging from privatization to increased taxation. But it cannot limit the opposition's freedom of expression, of self-organization, it cannot limit its access to mainstream and alternative media channels and, more important, cannot defend the opposition to run for mandates in regular elections. From this perspective, free and fair elections are to be seen as the most valuable political resource of the opposition. In fact, electoral fairness is the essential, yet only the first feature of a democratic system (Dahl 1971). Many countries are classified as electoral democracies in that they do not exceed this basic requirement, which is free and fair elections.

In Central and Eastern Europe, the democratic backsliding labeled here as post-accession hooliganism is defined as bending previously implemented democratic rules. By this, the democratization process is no longer a linear and ascending accumulation of democratic characteristics, but an unstable and reversible trend. This is true for various governments' attempts, in Poland and Hungary for instance, to consolidate in power by controlling mass media, changing the institutional design and limiting the judicial branch competences, and especially those of the Constitutional Court. Hungary has gone a very steep downward slope, since when the governing party FIDESZ has systematically been taking over the country's independent institutions, the presidency, the state audit office and the media council, only to give an example of a party in government interested to limit the democratic accountability (Agh 2014, 2015). Since the 2010 electoral victory for FIDESZ, Hungary has become a defective democracy. However, not even in Hungary the governing party looked for solutions aimed at limiting the opposition's chances of being elected, closing the democratic system and remaining in power only by authoritarian means, despite favorable changes in the electoral system. In Romania, however, the PDL government firmly decided to get rid of the basic accountability check, which are free and fair elections.

Evoking budgetary cuts of almost 20 million euros, figure that has to be compared with the consolidated budget for 2012 estimated at 45 billion euros, PDL decided in December 2011 to postpone local elections that had to be democratically held in June 2012 and to hold them at the same time with the parliamentary elections in December 2012 or in spring 2013. Moreover, the method used for passing the law in parliament is relevant for the political domination model endorsed by populists, which tends to exclude any legitimate contestation. In order to avoid any parliamentary debate on the issue, the government run by

PDL president, the prime minister Emil Boc, decided to endorse the law by engaging its responsibility. As mentioned before, this constitutional procedure enables, in fact, the government to automatically turn any proposal into effective law if the opposition in parliament does not demand for a confidence vote or if such a vote is rejected by the majority. On the contrary, a vote of confidence that fails automatically implies the fall of the government and the rejection of the proposal.

Why would a governing party, who has a political majority in parliament, intending to alter the rules of the game six months before the scheduled elections? In fact, local elections are critical for parties in Romania. On the one hand, as they generally have place six months before the parliamentary elections, their results act as benchmarks for the performance of political parties. In the Romanian context, marked by a deep distrust regarding pre-electoral surveys, local elections' results clearly indicate the strength of parties and almost accurately anticipate the parliamentary elections' results. This is especially the case of the elections for the county councilors and for the presidents of the county councils, which are the most 'political' elections. Unlike county elections, the local elections for commune and town councils and especially those for the mayors are to be considered as the most 'utilitarian', in Downsian terms, since voters' actions are rational in pursuing utility, i.e., that each citizen casts his vote for the mayoral candidate he believes will provide him with more benefits than any other (Downs 1957). Comparing county and parliamentary elections would give the opposition a clue about the ruling party's strength and help it in running the general campaign.

On the other hand, local elected officials in Romania often can work as electoral agents for their parties. By controlling local resources, especially in poorer rural areas, they usually discriminatorily provide citizens with various resources and facilities, from crop aids and timber supply to aids in cash, forcing them to electorally behave appropriately. Since half of the Romanian peasants are engaged in subsistence farming, they have been almost entirely 'captured' by local predatory elites who control resources and therefore local politics (Mungiu-Pippidi 2003). This strict dependency is strengthened in Romania by the governmental redistribution mechanisms. Designed to help local authorities to overcome unexpected difficulties and, more generally, to bridge development disparities (Dragoman 2011a), central government disposable funds and fiscal equalization funds were never free of political purposes. Whereas the central government may transfer equalization funds to counties, by taking for example into account their fiscal capacity to collect personal income tax or their stringent development needs, county councils may in turn distribute equalization funds to local communities inside counties. Controlling the central government and controlling as many county councils may provide the suitable tool to control the very local politics and influence voting, especially in backward rural communities confronted with harsh economic difficulties. Mixing local and parliamentary elections would make impossible a rebellion of local elected officials who might find an incentive to migrate towards the ranks of the most probable winner party in the subsequent parliamentary elections. By doing so, PDL expected to more tightly control its own local elected officials and to more effectively spend local resources for electoral purposes. Contested by the opposition, the law was in the end overruled by the Constitutional court. When ultimately held in June 2012, the local elections were largely won by the opposition, clearly anticipating the severe defeat of the PDL ruling party in the general elections held in December 2012.

Although postponing local elections would have saved 20 million euros and most probably offered PDL a mere electoral advantage, this measure would have seriously undermined democracy in terms of mechanism and resources. As mentioned above in this chapter, Downs (1957) emphasizes that in order to keep the rationality of both political system and political actors, the key condition is the fair and limited action of those in power and in opposition, i.e., the liberty of the government of disposing of economic resources for various policies that bring popular electoral support, yet limiting its action in restricting opposition's access to politically meaningful resources, including elections. Suspending or postponing elections actually prevent unsatisfied citizens to freely express political choices and the opposition to benefit of citizens' support. This may explain the outburst of public criticism, street protests and urban violence in January 2012, as emphasized in the next chapter, when the government decided to pass a controversial new law on public health by assuming its responsibility for the 14th time on a row. Moreover, PDL's intention to postpone local elections in order to alter the rules of the game and gain political advantages, especially by exploring unorthodox means to reduce its expected electoral losses, was clearly underlined by the 2012 Freedom House Nations in Transit Report as a very concerning issue, fully motivating its decision to downgrade Romania's score reflecting the electoral process in 2011 (Ştefan and Ioniţă 2012). The inactivity of organized civil society in contesting and containing the non-democratic practices of populists in 2012 and the action of less organized street protesters are the topic of the next chapter. It makes proof of the limits of democratization, especially when civil society action is tempered by a strong ideological anesthetic, and it offers new insights on the protest as a novel form of political participation in Romania.

7 Unpopular populists: public overt contestation and political survival strategies

Populists in Romania made consistent efforts to undermine the parliament in order to consolidate in power between 2008 and 2012. As representative body, the parliament was in the perception of populists competing for the privilege to speak for the people. In fact, populists claim to speak for the real people and to fight its enemies, which are most often imaginary rather than real. In this bitter fight against elites, depicted as corrupt, irresponsive and rigged against ordinary people, they recruit uniformed persons with no clear political preferences and who look for emotional rather than programmatic political satisfactions. Populists identify those elites in the same way they identify aliens and alien powers as scapegoats for their own political failures (Schmitter 2007).

Undermining the parliament was, for instance, in line with a more general development of the political system in Romania, which turned from a more consensual type of system in the early stage of transition towards a more majoritarian type. From this perspective, the institutional crises that occurred in Romania and the conflicts between the president Băsescu and prime ministers from the opposition parties which ended with the impeachment attempts in 2007 and 2012 can be seen as inherent to the ambiguous separation of powers induced by the malfunctioning of semi-presidential regimes, as it was the case in other countries in Eastern Europe (Protsyk 2005b; De Raadt 2009). On a closer scrutiny, it is visible that populists started by promising a bitter fight against endemic corruption and state institutions' inefficiency, under the banner of state reinvigoration, modernization and constitutional reform, but ended in a fight against competing sources of legitimacy and against the opposition and its political resources (Dragoman 2013). The parliament went under the verbal attack of populists, who built their whole campaign in 2007 for supporting the president Băsescu during the impeachment procedure by attacking the 322 deputies who voted for president's suspension from office. Moreover, in 2012, they labeled the second impeachment as a real coup and alerted the EU institutions and EU countries' embassies, warning for the alleged democratic setback. Although those verbal attacks could be taken for no more than current political issues, they in fact prepared the ground for more serious institutional changes.

In practice, the populists in government spared no effort to undermine the parliament by the excessive and unbalanced use of executive power. It is worth to remember that the PDL cabinet headed by Emil Boc flooded the parliament's agenda with emergency ordinances, forcing him to put deputies' initiatives on hold. Moreover, the prime minister Emil Boc largely abused of his constitutional right to adopt laws by engaging government's responsibility in parliament and thus regulated essential political domains with no parliamentary and public debate. In line with other attempts to strengthen the executive power and with PDL cabinet's decision in 2011 to postpone regular elections scheduled for 2012, they raised the fear of a decisive undemocratic backsliding (Dragoman and Gheorghiță 2013). These attacks against parliament are more than politics as usual. Institutional weakness, as noticed in Hungary and Poland in recent years, may seriously damage democratization. With an inchoate party system and a meager civil society, irrationalism, anti-elitism and xenophobia against aliens depicted as scapegoats for various political failures could only prepare the ground for more radical action.

7.1 Right-wing intellectuals and civil society apathy

We insist at the beginning of this chapter on the danger raised by de-democratization and the perils brought in by defective democracies in the region in order to tackle the issue of apathetic civil society. When confronted with current dangers and, furthermore, with plausible worse scenarios than the general backsliding, civil society remained unexpectedly silent. Although it was a key player and provided essential democratic resources during the initial phase of democratization, civil society refused to play a similar role when populists consolidated in power. Its apathy let the entire burden of the democratic contestation on the shoulders on less organized people in the streets. As emphasized in this chapter, this strange behavior marks the limits of the civil society as it was conceived in the early 1990s and brings in a new type of political action, which is protest. Before turning to street protests against populists, let us first examine the role played by the passive civil society during the populist domination between 2008 and 2012. The lack of action by civil society, which have could moderate populist actions, only encouraged populists to take undemocratic measures that turned them very unpopular. Combined with the distrust raised by numerous high-level official corruption scandals, the loss in popularity only consolidated the Romanian paradox of unpopular populists.

The apathy of the civil society is to be partially explained by ideological compatibility. This is not to say that the most prominent members of the civil society unconditionally supported populists in power, but to underline the special context where the virulent verbal anti-communism of the right-wing populists worked as an anesthetic for previously active members of the civil society. Therefore, civil society apathy could be explained through the lens of the ideological compatibility in two distinct ways. On the one hand, the willingness of many intellectuals forming the civil society to be part of the project of changing the society, to get coopted by political parties in a large scale transformation of institutions, economy and ideology. On the other hand, for many years following the 1989 revolution, right-wing intellectuals looked for a political force able to produce transitional justice, moral reparation and even lustration for those who previously have been communist party members. It is worth mentioning that in the aftermath of communism collapse in 1989, the intellectual debate in Eastern Europe started with the examination of the role played by communist ideology in supporting the authoritarian communist regime. In this vein, some scholars viewed intellectuals as valuable actors of democratization by creating debate, cultivating the alternative, breaking down stereotypes, relentlessly challenging thinking patterns, and facilitating public deliberations (Preoteasa 2002; Tănăsoiu 2008). As Tănăsoiu (2008) argues, Romanian intellectuals successfully managed after 1989 to provide the background for the emergence of a constructive discourse, which is pro-European and democratic. For many intellectuals forming the civil society, the two ways of ideological compatibility with populists in power worked hand in hand, their shared ideology combining with executive or counselor positions into state administration, including the Romanian Presidency.

Despite the importance of their social roles and even despite their democratic and pro-European discourse, Romanians right-wing intellectuals endorsed very seriously their task of attacking dogma and orthodoxy, deconstructing communist and national-communist narratives and challenging the previous evidence and ideology. They took it so seriously that they largely inhibited responses from left wing intellectuals. This become especially true when their virulent and obstinate struggle was conceived as not only to attack totalitarian style communism, but equally general left values. Consequently, the intellectual field is today ideologically largely dominated by ultra-liberalism, with no counterbalance from any left discourses. Therefore, one might actually doubt about the role that intellectuals have effectively played in developing a democratic political culture and in educating both the public and the political elites in the values of dialogue, compromise and civility, as Tănăsoiu (2008) argues. Instead of consolidating the public space by engaging in a dialogue, Romanian neo-liberal top intellectuals have rather symbolically appropriated public space and monopolized essential topics as democracy, civil society, reform and social justice.

7.1.1 Right-wing intellectuals on the road to power

Why ended Marxism so abruptly? What are the consequences for the functioning of the civil society in Romania? The quick answer is that nobody really believed in Marxism, so that is why it vanished immediately after 1989. But another explanation points towards the role played by right-wing intellectuals in supporting what Przeworski (1991) labelled as the greatest ideologically inspired experiment since Stalin's forced industrialization of the Soviet Union at the end of the 1920s. When the famous book by Konrád and Szelényi (1979) on the class structure of East European societies was published, in a certain respect as a response to Milovan Djilas's book on *The New Class* (1957), many sociologists believed that socialist states would finally and inevitably be dominated by a new class of bureaucrats and experts, who would use their indispensable knowledge to seize power and to further their own interests (Frentzel-Zagórska and Zagórski 1989). Although the dream of a *New Class* project still mesmerized East European intellectuals during the 1980s (Szelényi 1987), later on, following the collapse of communism, it was clear that social change was to be done not by intellectuals as a class, but by intellectuals as supporters of capitalist ideology and new capitalist entrepreneurs. Their effort was soon proving successful, as the new capitalist economy, the so-called capitalism without capitalists, was established by the former managerial elite, with the support of the new political elite (Eyal, Szelényi and Townsley 2001; Mink and Szurek 2002; Stoica 2004). After their successful anti-communist dissidence, post-communist intellectuals managed to help the radical capitalist change not only by intellectually legitimizing neo-liberalism, but also by severely criticizing alternative ideologies, especially socialism. This is why right-wing intellectuals supported right-wing parties willing to dramatically change society and politics in neo-liberal fashion, after a period when post-communist elites were reluctant in turning from pure communism to pure and harsh neo-liberalism.

This may therefore explain why Marxism vanished so quickly and left nothing behind. In fact, thirty years ago Marxism still completely influenced ideas, economy and politics and communism was a lived system of ideas. Whereas it still partially works in Russia (Dawisha 2005; Mayer and Küttner 2008; Sofronov 2008), and this despite the revisions in the late 1980s (Chafetz 1992), it ceased to have any impact on the post-communist world anywhere else. In Bulgaria, for example, the Marxist discourse has no place whatsoever in present public debates. It has been successfully substituted by a broad range of variants of a market-capitalistic talk, so successfully indeed that nobody questions the necessity of private property and initiative, markets (at least at some extent), different political parties or competition and all debates are strictly within the framework of democratization with marketization (Ganev 2005). In Ukraine, a powerful and widespread meta-narrative states that there is no alternative to neo-liberal capitalism (Williams and Round 2008). In Poland, even intelligentsia demonstrated exceptional imbecility in convincing itself of this proposition (Pinior 2007).

This is the general intellectual environment of early post-communist transition that largely shaped the political competition in Romania. Here, more than in other Central and East European country, the ideological debate was essential in guiding political strategies, as emphasized earlier in this volume. Unlike other countries in the region, which have been ruled by clear anti-communist governments immediately after 1989, Romania was trapped in a fierce political and ideological conflict between the former top communist party officials, then regrouped into a democratic and "revolutionary" party, and an intellectual and political right-wing opposition (Pop-Eleches 2008). In a sense, Romania faced an unfinished revolution by opposing a strong former communist party elite in power and a quite weak right-wing political opposition, yet firmly backed by a strong intellectual neo-liberal and conservative coalition (Roper 2004).

The peculiarity of the post-communist transformation in Romania is therefore a rather more intellectual and ideological than political opposition to power elites, namely an emphasis on perceived high values and benefits of neo-liberalism when compared to the economic failures and mass-murders of Marxist communism. This 'long-run' revolution that started in 1989 ended only in 1996 by a so-called electoral revolution, when a self-defined pro-Western coalition, led by an anti-communist intellectual, won against the incumbent president and former communist official Ion Iliescu, labeled as "an old *apparatchik*" (Roper and Feşnic 2003). Supporting PDL and Traian Băsescu in 2004 and 2008 for their promises for deep neo-liberal change was, therefore, much more comfortable for right-wing intellectuals than criticizing PSD and Ion Iliescu during the fragile and incipient capitalism in the early 1990s. Despite only few right-wing intellectuals got actually coopted by the right-wing populist party, the ideological compatibility expressed by numerous right-wing intellectuals worked as a powerful anesthetic for civil society. Their ideological support for PDL only increased when Traian Băsescu, as president of Romania, officially condemned communism.

7.1.2 Condemning the communist ideology, but not the communist oppressors

During the struggle of the 'unfinished revolution', sometimes taken for a 'quasi-revolution' (Tismaneanu 1993), the virulent anti-communist discourse of the intellectual counter-elites was the real political weapon of the opposition. Their anti-communist criticism ranges from symbolic to political, social, economic and even more personal issues. The first target of right-wing intellectual criticism was formed by the former communists themselves, actually labeled as 'neo-communists', and their alleged personal responsibilities for the misconduct of the former communist regime (Stan 2006). Whereas some countries decided to forgive and forget the former communists that perpetrated abuses, other countries have chosen to punish and prosecute those perpetrators. A series of states, like Hungary, took the middle road and effected only limited transitional justice (Stan 2007). In Romania, lustration and the official condemnation of the communist regime were at the heart of the political struggle between the former communists in power and the right-wing intellectual opposition in the early 1990s (Ciobanu 2009).

Whereas Romania took no decision in order to punish former communist officials, it was nevertheless decided that citizens could have access to files compiled by *Securitate*, the communist secret police. The Parliament set up in 2000 a Council for the Study of Securitate Archives in charge of *Securitate* files that facilitate citizens' access, states whether a person has collaborated with the former secret police and offers valuable information about the structure and functioning of *Securitate* (Stan 2004). It was a measure hailed by right-wing intellectuals who were arguing for the necessity of moral purification from past repression and the 'empires of lies' of the communist regime (Ciobanu 2009). Although Romania has not adopted a lustration policy, the Romanian President Traian Băsescu officially condemned communism by endorsing in 2007 a report issued by the Presidential Commission for the Analysis of the Communist Dictatorship in Romania (the so-called 'Truth Commission'), which was headed by Vladimir Tismăneanu (King and Sum 2011). In the end, this move was never followed by real measures against former highly ranked communist party members or against the top leaders of *Securitate*. They benefit, for example, of consistent pensions in accordance with their past activities or run successful private businesses.

The lack of distinctiveness between the crimes of the communist regime and the ideological content of communism, which is to be noticed when condemning communism as criminal ideology, is to be also found in the 'medical' approach used by right-wing intellectuals. In the early 1990s, they accused the Romanian society of being infected with some kind of a disgraceful disease, which is communism. Many right-wing intellectuals considered themselves as 'doctors' acting for the spiritual healing of the whole society. Gabriel Liiceanu, a prominent leader of the civil society, even made an appeal to all former communist party members and intellectual Marxists, labelled as 'scum people', to step out from their political and administrative functions and keep away from public office for a period, in order to purify and heal Romanian society from communism (Liiceanu 1992). Cited by Tănăsoiu (2008), Liiceanu's 'medical' mission sounds like this:

"The path we chose [. . .] cannot be one of material gain, but of a mission, a difficult path, noble and risky; this mission is of healing, during the years to come, the spirit of a society emerging from the dark of history."

For right-wing intellectuals, communism, alongside Nazism, is no less than a crime against humanity, and Marxist ideology cannot be successfully separated to this crime, as it is its very origin. The current tendencies of exonerating Marxism and communism for past crimes and intellectually rehabilitate them are inacceptable for Patapievici (1996, 213). Therefore, not only communist criminals should be chased and prosecuted, but one should use the penal code when dealing with Communism and Nazism as political ideologies. The opinions shared by the two prominent right-wing intellectuals are much telling about the intellectual and ideological environment of the early 1990s. Facing former communist party members, who were reluctant to put in place clear marketization and lustration measures, public intellectuals grouped together under the umbrella of the *Group for Social Dialogue* (Grupul pentru Dialog Social – GDS) and of the right-wing party *Civic Alliance* (Alianţa Civică – AC). They formed the very core of the political opposition that managed to electorally defeat PDSR back in 1996 and to push for neo-liberal policies. With the rapid consolidation of capitalism, their final political project was to condemn communism. This is why right-wing intellectuals remained silent when populists turned from reinvigorating state institutions and fighting corruption to political actions aimed at consolidating in power with all costs. Public intellectuals' apathy opened the door to a new form of political action, namely protest. There were people in the streets who represented the last democratic resource. Their successful fight against populism in power, with no help from the more organized civil society associations, marks the end of the democratization through voluntary associations and sets the stage for mass mobilization of more diverse, disparate and fragmented groups. The changing pattern in political action signals the coming of a new democratic development stage, under the impact of changing models of mass communication, new media and social networks, as we underline in the next chapter.

7.2 Unpopular populists: facing overt public contestation

Right-wing intellectuals' apathy in relation with the undemocratic moves of the populists in power points towards a special ideological relationship and unravels possible consequences on the long and short term. On the long run, the ultra-dominance of neo-liberalism might seriously affect the consolidation of a public space, a public sphere that serves as prerequisite for a functional democracy and for a cohesive society. Such a public sphere is an environment accepting the public political reasoning, an environment in which the individual can speak freely and where the arguments are not influenced by any political or social power. It makes possible for everyone to express himself, regardless of any constraints on time, resources, participation or themes (Habermas 1989), as emphasized earlier in this volume.

There are two perspectives on the generation of the public space. If one is to conceive public space as a given empty space, where hostile forces compete for domination, then communism is banned today due to the failure of communism as a functional economic and political system. The disposable public space is therefore monopolized by neo-liberalism, which works as the only game in town. If one conceives public space as generated by the free interaction between independent actors, as Habermas (1989) suggests, then the reluctance of left-wing intellectuals to compete for public space is a guarantee for the dominance of right-wing ideas in a close and hostile environment. This hostile environment disables any exchange of ideas and, therefore, inhibits any development of a genuine public sphere. In other words, the lack of interaction between ideas undermines any functional public space, leading to uncontested right-wing ideology and propaganda instead of competing arguments.

The malfunctioning of the public space in Romania has already been noticed with great accuracy by Patapievici (2007). He emphasizes the importance of the intricate and bivariate relationship between objective communication and the public space. Patapievici starts from the discursive functions of the public space in order to explain the lack of specialized markets of ideas in almost every cultural and scientific sub-field in Romania. But he easily extends those observations to the more general conditions in society. It seems that the market of ideas is missing in Romania because there is no general, and not only specific, public space. According to Peirce, quoted by Patapievici (2007, 77), objectivity and community are strongly related. As stated by Peirce, whose writings have been edited by Hartshorne and Weiss (1934), 'the opinion which is fated to be ultimately agreed to by all who investigate, is what we mean by true, and the object represented in that opinion is real' [therefore] 'the very origin of the conception of reality shows that this conception essentially involves the notion of community'. With no common interest, there is no community. A free market (of any kind of exchanges, including those of ideas), is therefore a prerequisite for any community. Individuals' awareness of living in a unified reality comes from the full functioning of the community they belong to (Patapievici 2007,

105). Embracing neo-liberalism as the only game in town may avoid intellectual competition, but could distort reality and undermine community.

7.2.1 Neo-liberalism and the economic crisis of 2010

The short term effect of civil society reluctance to challenge right-wing populists in power could be visible in populists' readiness for profound neo-liberal political and economic actions. With no public critiques from the established civil society, populists shown little moderation in controlling political resources and exploiting state resources. Harsh anti-social measures, combined with a severe neo-liberal approach in tackling the economic crisis in 2010, turned populists in power very unpopular. This first explanation of their sudden unpopularity is to be added to the second one, which is pervasive high-level corruption. Their combination opened the door to one of the most serious popular contestations after 1989.

The total lack of criticism from civil society only encouraged the ultra-liberal government to adopt in 2010 harsh social and economic measures, including a severe 25% cut in all public salaries and an additional 16% tax on pensions, but also to massively reduce the social benefits of families with children, as well as of elderly and disabled people. At the same time, the right-wing government decided to raise the VAT with 25% (from 19 to 24%). Those measures were publically defended by right-wing populists by opposing a catastrophically depicted alternative, which would have been to abandon the 16% flat tax on all revenues and increase taxation.

This neo-liberal move was made by the Liberal Democrat Party in total contradiction with its 2008 electoral promises, based on very generous social and economic measures. Although the economic picture of the 2010 crisis in Romania is more complex than this, the response of the government is much telling about its ideological orientation. When confronted with economic troubles and forecasting smaller public revenues, the government strongly supported big entrepreneurs and especially banks. Abruptly increasing VAT with 25% meant placing the fiscal burden on the shoulders on every single individual, who faced increasing prices for goods and services. Reducing the salaries of all public employees with 25%, but also of those people working in the public sector, ranging from firefighters and bus drivers to teachers and hospital doctors, only increased the fiscal burden on many ordinary people. Additionally, a public loan of 20 billion dollars has been contracted from the International Monetary Fund for supporting private banks in Romania. Keeping in place the 16% flat tax on revenues, alongside fueling commercial banks with public money, was

the strongest commitment assumed by the PDL government to support the private capital and business. Even if this option was conditioned by its ideological
orientation, in that affecting capital would have meant disobeying long-lasting
moral and political commitments, the plummeting popularity would have been
impossible without increasing corruption. The reduction in public salaries and
the severe cuts in social benefits, which were in many cases less than satisfactory
even before the drastic cuts, did not trigger street protests. Unexpectedly, the
Romanian public accepted the cuts with resignation. It was only the political
abuse, as emphasized below, that set the fire and provoked the protest outburst.

7.2.2 Unpopular populists and large-scale high-level corruption

The issue of corruption was one of the key issues in PDL's electoral campaigns in
2004 and 2008-2009. Accusing the incumbent PSD party candidates, and especially its party president and presidential candidate Adrian Năstase of corruption was in line with populists' political action of fighting corrupt political elites,
depicted as arrogant, despising and rigged against ordinary people. Speaking
for the people, and subsequent to the electoral victory working for the people,
was also fighting corruption among political opposition's ranks. Băsescu's and
PDL's campaign slogans were aimed at mobilizing ordinary people by violent
yet suggestive images. The people was called to action, to "impale" and "burn"
corrupt officials, in order to finally topple down communism perpetuated by
the prolonged rulership of PDSR. The violent mobilization was recalling the
method used by Vlad Țepeș (Vlad the Impaler) to punish theft and corruption
(Dragoman and Ungureanu 2017).

Despite the much awaited state institutions' reinvigoration, increasing
accountability and institutional performance, once in government PDL only continued to colonize public offices with unqualified, yet obedient party members.
Replacing public servants in office was taken for a guarantee in implementing
decisive action in modernizing the state. In fact, state modernization become
one of the most frequent slogans used by Traian Băsescu and PDL in order to
justify political changes. Replacing public servants with party members is one
of the most common features of post-accession hooliganism in Central and
Eastern Europe. In Romania however, populists' electoral promises for honest
and responsible young politicians and public servants raised very high expectations, in contradiction with the quality of young people promoted by Traian
Băsescu and PDL in various public offices.

But the most contrasting issue when comparing the electoral campaign
promises and slogans with the effective exercise of state authority following

successful elections is corruption. Although corruption is generally measured by the subjective perception on the matter, numerous cases of high-level corruption which have been investigated after 2012 confirm the perception people had during populists' rule. The Transparency International Corruption Perception Index for Romania, a sociological indicator for the subjective level of corruption experienced by the citizens of a given country, indicates serious setbacks in 2011 and 2010, comparing with 2009 and 2008. This measure was to strengthen the overall perception of independent journalists and experts who were dealing with corruption cases. This was not only the much controversial corruption case of the minister of Youth and Sports from the PDL government (Ştefan, Tapalagă and Ioniţă 2010). It was even the European Commission who decided in 2012 to suspend payments for a great number of projects supervised by the Ministry of Regional Development and Tourism during the 2010–2011 period, due to serious financial misconducts.

The contrasting issue of corruption was in fact worsened by PDL's strategy to compensate the loss in direct social benefits by promising essential indirect benefits from huge public investments, some of them in relation with campaign promises made back in 2008. It is worth mentioning that before and during the 2008 electoral campaign, Theodor Stolojan, the PDL leader economist and former prime minister set up a number of targets for the governing period, including essential increase of public salaries from a mean of 450 up to 905 euro, of public pensions from a mean of 160 up to 405 euro and no less than 836 km of brand new highways. It was not only the economic crisis that disabled PDL to fulfill its promises, but also the pervasive corruption that oriented PDL strategy not to serious and sustainable public investments, but to quick material gain from useless and over-evaluated public investments projects. It was only after 2012 that prosecutors unraveled the huge scale of corruption, with hundreds of millions of euros from central and local budgets being oriented to private pockets, partly in order to finance the costly presidential campaign in 2009. Contrary to electoral promises to investigate dishonest public funding for big infrastructure projects made by PSD, as the project of a brand new highway in Transylvania, PDL continued to finance them. This led to one of the most striking paradoxes of their mandate, namely the payment for the projected highway which had to stretch from Braşov to Oradea (415 km), renegotiated in 2005 and 2011 and limited to only 112 km. The huge payment was finally done for only the 52 km of motor highway actually built. Although back in 2004 Traian Băsescu, then presidential candidate, accused the French Prime Minister Jean-François Raffarin of collusion with the Romanian Prime Minister in office Adrian Năstase, presidential candidate as well, to obtain illegal gains from commercial agreements between

France and Romania, once in office he did not oppose to the renegotiation of the contract and to the payment for the Transylvania highway. The financing was justified with the need for good transport infrastructure.

It was the same strategy when cutting the social aid for supporting mothers with children under the age of two. Back in 2010, when severe social cuts have been promoted, PDL promised a strong increase in the construction of new kinder gardens. When PDL government decided to close down dozens of public hospitals in 2011, he promised to turn every single hospital into a special unit for elderly care. In the spring 2012, when the PDL government was dismissed by the parliament, there were hardly a couple of new kinder gardens and a few hospitals turned into social care units and less than 100 km of motor highways. The investments were turned instead into very controversial and costly projects of sport and tourist facilities, including a new tourist national branding campaign and several football pitches in rural country side. No green-field general hospitals or significant brand new sport arenas were actually built.

The end of populists' rule in 2012 opened the door to important judicial inquiries. Until that moment, the only case investigated was that of the minister of Youth and Sports, mentioned earlier in this chapter. Despite some accusations related to high-level corruption and the illegal funding of PDL's electoral campaigns have been made during PDL's mandate, the scale of the governmental corruption was unraveled after 2012 and especially after 2014, when Traian Băsescu was replaced by Klaus Johannis as president of Romania. The prosecutors from the Anti-Corruption Directorate (Direcția Națională Anticorupție – DNA) and those from the General Prosecutor's Office in charge with investigating organized crime and terrorism (Direcția de Investigare a Infracțiunilor de Crimă Organizată și Terorism – DIICOT) launched a series of investigations against high-level PDL officials, PDL ministers from the Emil Boc cabinet, PDL deputies and mayors, including close friends and collaborators of the former president Traian Băsescu. They have been charged of bribery, fraud, abuse and illegal personal gains. The investigated cases concerned important amounts of money, coming from commercial contracts with big companies as Microsoft. Some of the convicted, as for example the former Communication minister Gabriel Sandu, acknowledged the misdeed and indicated that the destination of the money obtained by fraud was PDL, always in need for its very costly electoral campaigns. Elena Udrea, a close collaborator of Traian Băsescu and former Regional Development minister in the same PDL cabinet, confirmed the same destination of many briberies, some of them perpetrated by Alin Cocoș, her own husband. Although some of the accusations failed to be probated in court, as for example those against Ion Ariton, the Industry minister in

PDL cabinet, many of the accusations have been finally probated. The financial scale of the high-level corruption, involving hundreds of millions of euros, and the many dozens of years of prison cumulated by the convicted make proof of the terrifying level of governmental corruption during PDL rule.

7.3 Street protests and the dismissal of the PDL government

Benefitting of the unconditional support of the right-wing intellectuals, the government faced no intellectual critique and had only to defend himself against contestation in the street, which he addressed by pure police force (Stoica 2012). Contrary to what one could have expected when noticing the unusually severe cuts in social benefits in 2010 and the serious economic contraction (-7.1% in 2009 and -0.8% in 2010) that preceded those harsh measures, the contestation of the PDL government headed by Emil Boc was not due to anti-social measures, but merely to political abuse. Entrenched in a neo-liberal strategy of reducing public services in order to cut budgets negotiated with IMF, the PDL government managed in Spring 2011 to close down more than 60 second-order public hospitals from numerous counties, with the promise to turn them later into elderly people care facilities, as mentioned before.

Noticing the meager public opposition to previous efforts to reduce public spending, PDL and Traian Băsescu tried to further reduce and eventually privatize the emergency care sector in Romania. They intended to extend the private companies right to treat emergency patients. Until 2011 they were allowed to treat patients only at home. Extending homecare to street care, giving those private companies the permission to treat accident casualties, for example, would have encouraged them to invest into private ambulances and private emergency hospitals, turning emergency services into commercial business. Raed Arafat, a state secretary in the Public Health Ministry overtly contested the decision elaborated by a special presidential health care commission. His strong opposition to PDL's project made Traian Băsescu enter live into a televised debate and announce the *ad hoc* dismissal of the state secretary. The abuse was evident. As president of Romania, Traian Băsescu had no competence in dismissing a state secretary. Moreover, his virulent attempt to silence critics opposing his discretionary measures trigger an unexpected outburst of protest. Thousands of citizens took to the streets in order to defend and support the state secretary, who was well known in Romania for his effort in consolidating the emergency integrated health care service in the early 1990s (Serviciul Mobil de Urgenţă, Reanimare şi Descarcerare – SMURD). The highly operative emergency service was already implemented in many Romanian counties and had helped saving numerous lives. Due to this very sensitive issue, the emotion generated by the unfair and abusive dismissal turned into overt street contestation in January 2012. Initially started in Târgu-Mureş, the Transylvanian town where Raed Arafat put in place since 1992 the SMURD service, the contention spread throughout the country, reaching big and medium-size cities.

The overt contestation in Târgu-Mureş in January 2012 marks the beginning of the end of populists' rule. With people in the street demanding cabinet and president's resignation, the populists have entered the most awkward political situation, in that populists in power have become truly unpopular. Although the theoretical approach about unpopular populists is intriguing, what we try to unravel here is the way populists coped with the contestation and how they managed to save as many power positions. At the end of the contestation period, their exit from power let them weakened, but still capable of defending some key positions.

Facing overt popular contestation, the first strategy was to despise the critics by labeling them as minor, irrelevant and strange people, on the one hand, or insidious enemies from within, on the other hand. This strategy was not new. It was used to divide the people by publically unmasking a bitter enemy from within in 2010, in order to justify the drastic cuts in salaries and pensions. Those to be pinpointed as enemies were employees in the public sector, who constituted an unfair burden on the shoulders of the private sector. The enemies who were previously external to the people, namely corrupt elites and sinister interest groups, are now internal: doctors and nurses who unfairly demand higher salaries instead of leaving the country and working hard in foreign hospitals, teachers from Romanian schools who were producing but idiot graduates, desperate mothers with babies in their arms crying for unfair social benefits. None of them deserve to benefit from public support, since they are not socially significant. Moreover, the leader of PDL deputies Mircea Toader, declared that all people killed by blizzard in one of the worse snowfalls in winter 2012 were no more than miserable drunk men.

The second strategy was to try to diminish the scale of the contestation, according to the people a minor role. Whereas back in 2004 and 2008, populists were speaking for the people and their whole legitimacy was based on the will of the people, in 2012 the popular contestation was but a political weapon of the opposition. The strategy is to be noticed in the evaluation of the contestation directed against Traian Băsescu. What 'people' really means for populists, since people do not longer support populists in office? Back in 2007, the president Băsescu was put back in office by people voting 'no' to the referendum for dismissal, with no concern regarding the participation threshold. In order to secure his second presidential mandate, as emphasized before, PDL majority in parliament voted a change to the law regarding the referendum and imposed an absolute majority as threshold for the referendum's validation. For then on, it would be enough for a president to be elected by a simple majority, but not enough to be dismissed. The legitimacy of the president can derive from a simple majority, yet the people are not legitimate to remove the same president from office unless it converges into a qualified majority. Although this issue could be seen as a banal institutional arrangement which is part of the overall institutional design, what lies at the heart of this issue is the definition of 'people' and its importance for unpopular populists.

When the parliament suspended the president Traian Băsescu for the second time, in regular plenary session in 2012, he condemned the move and labeled it as a coup. Despite protests from some European officials and politicians from several EU states who embraced the allegations, the president was forced to confront the real people. Before parliament's decision, he made an appeal to his electorate to keep supporting him and to vote 'no' into a future referendum, as they did back in 2007. He would have not desired to be put back in office by a Constitutional Court decision that would have invalidated the referendum, due to lack of qualified majority to the polls. When finally suspended, he made himself a televised appeal for boycotting of the referendum, labelling it as a sinister coup against democracy and Romania's European belonging.

As mentioned in the previous chapter, following the referendum that surprised by the large participation, compared to regular elections, the Constitutional Court decided that the presence was not sufficient enough and invalidated the referendum, putting the president Băsescu back in office. The Court founded its decision on an essential democratic question: who is the people? According to Sartori (1987), the people can be defined as the totality of citizens or as a majority, expressing accurately enough its sovereignty. In order to calculate the threshold majority, the Court decided to use the disposable public data of the 2002 general official census. Based on this benchmark, the presence acknowledged by the Court counted for only 46%. The Court refused to take into account any other legal, practical or sociological consideration, namely the severe demographic drop of the overall population and high figures of emigration, with millions of people setting their permanent residence in Western Europe, especially in Spain, Italy, France and Germany, making thus impossible to expect them to vote in large shares on a national referendum.

Although legal, the Court decision frustrated the overwhelming share of citizens voting for president's dismissal (more than 7,4 million people, almost 90% of those who voted) and shed new light on the relationship between populists and the real people. As emphasized by Sartori (1987), 'the demolatry' turns 'people' into a fiction, with no concern for the real people. Following the Court's final decision, the president Băsescu praised in an official televised statement the victory of the democracy and of those who did not express their views by refraining from voting. Moreover, he accused widespread irregularities in casting the ballots and pinpointed his adversaries' misconduct, who allegedly falsified no less than 2 million votes. The judicial subsequent tribulations, including penal inquiries against hundreds of peasants who were accused on electoral misconduct, are to be seen as president's struggle to overcome a democratic contradiction: how to safeguard legitimacy and to conciliate a 5.2 million vote in his favor back in 2009, with a crashing 7.4 million in favor of his dismissal in 2012.

The preservation of the presidential seat was accompanied by the limitation of the electoral defeat. Using electoral strategies of changing the district where they have been previously elected, and even changing their name and electoral colors by entering into an electoral alliance with smaller parties, Rightful Romania (Alianța România Dreaptă – ARD), PDL candidates managed to secure a narrow parliamentary representation. But the most successful strategy was in fact to block with a complaint to the Constitutional Court the new electoral law passed by the opposition Social Liberal Alliance (Uniunea Social Liberală – USL) formed by PSD and PNL. The new electoral law adopted in 2012 by USL would have instituted a pure majoritarian electoral system (FPTP). By its effect, which is a consistent disproportionality, FPTP would have over-represented USL and under-represented PDL. With plummeting voting sympathies, PDL would have been excluded from the parliamentary representation, due to the 5% threshold in place. Avoiding parliamentary exclusion was therefore the main target of populists' strategy. Moreover, their ability of changing the way of electing mayors would finally prove beneficial. Passing from a majoritarian two-rounds run-off (TR), or double ballot, to pure FPTP system in order to elect mayors has increased PDL candidates' chances of being elected. With no second round to face, with lower public exposure and with no absolute majority to gain, PDL candidates won mandates with fewer shares of votes that it was the case in 2008. Important mayoral seats have been won in big cities (Arad, Alba-Iulia, Brașov) with less than 50% of the votes. Moreover, Emil Boc, the former prime minister who resigned in February 2012 as a PDL attempt to clean its reputation, won the mayoral seat of the biggest city in Transylvania, Cluj-Napoca, with only 40.6% of the votes. The law regarding the election of mayors that he has been modified on purpose proved to be for Emil Boc a personal escape from a very unpopular mandate as prime minister. The interested legislator, as emphasized earlier, is one of the most striking characteristics of post-accession hooligans.

The resignation of Emil Boc as prime minister and the appointment of Mihai-Răzvan Ungureanu was not enough to clean PDL's tarnished political image. Fearing a disastrous electoral defeat, many PDL deputies and senators voted against their own government in April 2012, making the PDL government the second government dismissed by a no confidence vote in parliament after the adoption of the Constitution in 1991. By toppling their own cabinet, PDL deputies and senators retrenched into the opposition's ranks, leaving the room for the USL government headed by Victor Ponta. Following the success in maintaining parliamentary representation in December 2012 under the banner of ARD, the populist PDL finally merged in July 2014 with PNL after the dismantling of the alliance between PNL and PSD in February 2014. Although their political trajectory ended in the framework of the liberal party (PNL) and in opposition to PSD beginning with 2014, the dismissal of the PDL cabinet would have been improbable without the massive street contestation against PDL and the president Traian Băsescu. With no support from the civil society, street protesters ended by their own forces the political cycle of populism in power and opened the door to the consolidation of a new type of political action in Romania, namely to protest.

8 Twenty-five years of democratic transition and consolidation

The presidential elections in December 2014 brought in a huge surprise in Romanian politics. Klaus Werner Johannis, the PNL candidate, was elected president of Romania. He defeated the prime minister in office, the PSD candidate, Victor Ponta. The surprise was mainly due to Johannis political profile. Less visible that his opponent, Johannnis was for one decade and a half the mayor of Sibiu, a medium-sized town in Transylvania. Although he was previously proposed by PNL as prime minister candidate back in October 2009, after the dismissal by the parliament of the first Emil Boc cabinet, he had not the national visibility of the prime minister in office. Moreover, Johannis was for 25 years the president of the German Democratic Forum (Forumul Democrat al Germanilor din România – FDGR), a cultural association politically representing ethnic Germans in local, regional and national politics.

Active in a highly atypical political environment in Sibiu, where ethnic prejudices have been overpassed and the FGDR candidate was elected as mayor four times on a row (Zamfira and Dragoman 2009), Johannis managed to overpass prejudices at national level and won the electoral competition. It is worth mentioning that Johannis is a Catholic German, whereas the vast majority of Romania's citizens are ethnic Romanians of Orthodox faith. What seems to have helped him to overpass prejudice is his previous performance as Sibiu mayor, and especially his role in the designation of this town as European Capital of Culture in 2007. The success story of Sibiu as capital of culture helped balancing national identity with feelings of European pride and belonging (Dragoman 2008), in the very year of Romania's accession to the European Union. By emphasizing his European profile, his openness towards diversity and his administrative performance, Johannis managed to persuade those electors looking for a candidate capable of leading Romania towards institutional performance and stronger European integration, in both values and public policies domains.

From the perspective expressed in this volume, the election of Klaus Johannis puts an end to a long period of democratic transition. Despite its situation of laggard regarding the EU accession, the democratic trajectory of Romania is by no means different from that of other former socialist countries in Central and Eastern Europe. Electing a candidate differing in many respects from the average Romanian politician is much telling about citizens' commitment in supporting democratization and European integration. With comparable democratic trajectories with other countries in the region, Romania has entered in a democratic consolidation phase. The populist backlash has been however a tough episode in the course of the consolidation process. Despite the initial fears that citizens would be reluctant to a democratization that would bring in social costs and high personal uncertainty, Romania's democratic trajectory makes proof of a strong citizens' commitment. Not only that they did not support non-democratic alternatives, but they endured severe changes in their living conditions, facing economic deprivation, unemployment and the loss of the previous social safety net. Even during populists' rule between 2008 and 2012, people largely accepted the massive reduction in social benefits, including salary cuts of 25%. Their protest, which toppled populists in Spring 2012, marks the profound change in the repertories of political action. Democratic consolidation has brought in a new kind of political action, meaning that Romanian citizens seem to have burned stages of political participation and moved beyond the more classical forms of participation only to embrace protest.

8.1 Critical citizens: protests and new forms of political participation

The scale of protest and the dynamic of political participation open a new stage for democratic consolidation in Romania. As underlined in this final chapter, the change in the participation style of citizens, although influenced by changing conditions in mass communication due to the spread of new devices that are capable of keeping people connected and thus forming a virtual communication environment, may be the proof of a profound change in the participation model. As anticipated by Barnes (2004b), changing social conditions in post-communism could lead citizens of the former communist countries to burn stages of political development and to move to new, unconventional forms of participation, with no necessary passage through more classical, conventional styles of political action. If it is to be confirmed by separate and solid research results, this change would have an important impact on the way people conceive participation, empowerment and political accountability. Before turning to those consequences for the consolidation of democracy in Romania, let us first briefly discuss about the changing participation model.

8.1.1 Political activism and dominant social values

Being politically active means using its citizenship resources and taking part to the common duties. In terms of Verba, Schlozman and Brady (2000), political participation means more than voting, but incorporates all acts that are intended to have the consequence of influencing the choice of governing officials or the policies they make and implement. As mentioned in the chapter dedicated to the political participation style, participation has been evolving from simple, conventional forms as voting and working for political parties to new, unconventional forms, that is protest (Barnes and Kaase 1979). This essential change has accompanied a more profound change in dominant value system, with post-material values replacing older, material values (Inglehart 1977). This change was brought in by massive changes in mass education and communication. Generalized education and mass communication made less necessary for citizens to rely on political parties for political education and guidance on public policy areas and opened the door to a new kind of mobilization, which is cognitive mobilization (Barnes 2004a). With a range of new facilities for communication, with an impressive technical advance in communication devices as well, the citizens' exposure to information certainly led to a changing model of political activism. This is why we do have so many young people in the streets of big cities (Norris, Walgrave and van Aelst 2005).

Tested in the Romanian case, as mentioned earlier in the special chapter dedicated to the discussion about political participation, the increase in educational attainment and in income, as well as political interest, are strong predictors for protest. Those young people who display such characteristics tend to be more active, although it is hard to clearly assess a difference in post-material values. In other words, they are not more active on unconventional ground because they are more inclined towards post-material values, but mainly because there is a more general change in participation model. It does not mean that there are no politically active young people who express those values, who care about the environment, for example, but those values are not the essential explanation of their increased activism (Dragoman 2011b). What seems to count more is the mobilization strategy, facilitated by new means of mass communication.

8.1.2 Protest and the support for democracy

An essential question could be raised in the context of protest, namely the democratic or the anti-democratic orientation of protesters. It is worth remembering that contestation was generally seen for decades as an obstacle for stabilizing transitional regimes, stability being a prerequisite for economic development and growth (Huntington 1968). Moreover, in the context of democratization, communist regimes have been toppled with the essential participation of street protesters. Despite round-tables where power elites were confronted by counter-elites, street protesters represented the essential ally of those interested in putting an end to the communist rule. In Romania, for instance, where there were no round tables and the communist leader ruled until his very last days in a way that made the regime be labeled as sultanism (Linz and Stepan 1996), the victory of the revolution would have been impossible without the massive street protest. However, in the context of post-communism in Romania, protest has been used to challenge the democratic framework in early 1990s, when violent coal miners have been used as a weapon against the democratic opposition. In addition, protest may have deep social motivations, flagging the existence of a serious dissatisfaction with the general and more personal economic standards (Uslaner 2004). We have no data supporting the hypothesis of the democratic contestation by widespread protest, as mentioned previously. It rather seems that protesters emphasize the need for more freedom of expression and the rejection of authority. This is in line with the further developments in Romanian politics, which will be addressed below.

From another perspective, protest as a new mainstream form of political participation signals the challenge to the more conventional forms of participation. In the era of cognitive mobilization, with the facility of street gathering by new media channels, participation in voluntary organizations seems less necessary. It is especially true when it comes to take into account the democratic role played by those secondary associations. With a decrease in participation in those associations, protest remains the main form of political action. In the streets, there are also present those who were active a decade ago in voluntary associations, but the large number of those who protest overpasses the very limited participation in voluntary associations. This was visible in the scale of protests against PSD run governments in December 2015 and January 2017. In a way, democratization in Romania has overpassed the stage where those working and fighting for democratic consolidation were but a handful of civic activists, whose associations were funded by external pro-democratic funders and institutions.

8.2 Challenges and prospects for democracy in Romania

The "democratization" of the democratic contestation brought in large categories of previously apathetic young people. But it also put an end to the effective impact and the symbolic importance of civil society's most prominent associations and intellectuals. Their assumed partisanship and their incapacity to fight political abuse when coming from right-wing populist parties in power marks the end of the civil society as it was conceived during the initial phases of the democratic transition. Although civic associations and their leaders, public intellectuals, played a decisive role in containing post-communist successor parties' influence and action during the early stages of democratization, their tacit, unconditional support for right-wing populists made them lose their previous legitimate influence. Whereas some of their members have been coopted in various political functions, most of them in the presidential administration and in the diplomatic apparatus, the essential anesthetic came from the ideological compatibility with populists in power, especially from the official condemnation of communism by the president Traian Băsescu. This verbal action, in fact miles away from a coherent policy of transitional justice including or not lustration, was sufficient to silence critics from right-wing intellectuals and from previously highly praised voluntary organizations.

From the perspective opened by Konrád and Szelényi (1979), right-wing intellectuals' road to power ended in another illusion. Having in mind that capitalism and liberalism would be rebuilt after socialism with their essential contribution as a group, as they were indispensable for the new task of deep social change, it turned out that their only contribution would be to spread the right-wing political ideas. Although capitalism, full marketization and large-scale privatization have become the only game in town, the action and profit were in the hands of a new prosperous class, including many of the former managers of previously state-owned companies. They turned out to be even better capitalists that they were state managers. Therefore, the ideological compensation largely needed by right-wing intellectuals was exactly the official condemnation of communism as criminal ideology. Ironically, this compensation was finally provided not by genuine right-wing politicians, close allies of those intellectuals, politicians who won the 1996 elections against Ion Iliescu and PDSR, labeled as the orthodox successors of the former communist party. It was done by the leader of the party which officially inherited from the FSN, the revolutionary Front which succeeded to the communist party in the early days of the post-communist transition. It was done by Traian Băsescu, president of the populist PD, elected in 2004 as president of Romania. His much controversial professional career as chief of Romania's trade office in Antwerp during the last decades of the communist rule, a well remunerated commercial function but very close to Securitate's activities in Western Europe, raised little concern. What seems to have counted was the official condemnation of communism, taken as an ideological revenge and an incontestable proof of social and political domination.

With no support from public intellectuals, the democratic contestation against populists in power laid on the shoulders of ordinary protesters in the streets. The split between street democratic contestation and visible intellectual critique marks the end of civil society, as it was conceived in the early 1990s. In that period, the two actions worked hand in hand in limiting political abuse and putting pressure for a stronger pro-European orientation of the government. The legitimation of the street as unique relevant democratic actor opens a new era in political action, with two perspectives on the long run. The first perspective is a continually growing power of street rallies as the main mean of politically controlling the elected officials. This style of political action shortcuts any legitimate intermediate representative body, in order to face politicians with the consequences of their political decisions. Although it relates closely to what it is imagined as direct democracy, it may turn undemocratic if the street rallies miss their initial political target. In other words, any legitimate action could easily become immoderate and destructive. Or the moderation and the capacity to discriminate could be difficult tasks for people who do not form coherent groups, but simply gather in the streets following a mobilization action. In this vein, one could hardly distinguish between a genuine mobilization and a politically driven one, due to the fundamental incapacity of ordinary people to discriminate in a very short lap of time between legitimate and illegitimate demands.

Though cognitive mobilization offers for the first time the opportunity to get engaged by selecting from a very diverse range of causes and solicitations in terms of personal interest and passions (Barnes 2004a), the uninterrupted flux of communication, as well as the growing complexity of issues at stake make very difficult for an ordinary citizen to discriminate between true and false, relevant or irrelevant. Romania has recently witnessed two episodes of massive and strikingly rapid political mobilization. The first one was in November 2015 against the PSD government run by Victor Ponta, when the street protest ended with the resignation of the prime minister. The second one was in January 2017, when hundreds of thousands of people in the streets demanded the PSD government run by Sorin Grindeanu to redraw a very controversial change to the Penal Code that would had favored public functionaries and encourage them to perpetrate corrupt actions. Although the two protests ended by forcing elected officials to make a step backward, their political force and mobilizing capacity shed new light on the new democratic context in Romania. Not only this kind of political action leaves no space for dialogue and negotiation, which is specific to a democratic environment, but could easily be reoriented by forces that would intend to take over. Fake-news and even misunderstanding could mobilize social forces that would turn out to be very hard to demobilize, since those new forms of political participation are rather diffuse and do not acknowledge the authority of any leader. The confusion regarding the veracity of the failed military coup in Turkey in July 2016 is much telling about the difficulty one has to discriminate when emotions and interests mingle in the evaluation of a specific context or event. Speaking for the people, which is specific for the populists in power in Romania between 2008 and 2012, could thus pave the way for a more radical and irrational movement, with much heavier consequences for the still fragile democratic system in Romania. Ethnic, religious or just ideological differences could be successfully used in order to create enemies from within. Fighting those inner enemies could, in turn, justify any irrational authoritarian movement, as it is currently the case with Turkey since the alleged coup from July 2016.

The second perspective is a balance between growing direct democracy, made easier by the communication environment which can work as a virtual community, and a strong network of secondary organizations which form the backbone of a solid civil society. Associations may keep their role of schools of democracy (Putnam 1993), teaching the lessons of commitment, trust and tolerance for those engaged in political and social action. They might form civic activists who could become opinion leaders, spilling the benefits of getting engaged over the boundaries of their own associations. The spillover effect is possible only in a special environment, which is the public sphere.

As strongly emphasized in the previous chapter, public sphere is generated by the communication interaction (Habermas 1989) of those willing to let arguments to be decisive, instead of power that derives from status, wealth or any given authority. In this special environment, right-wing intellectuals have to refrain from power attitudes deriving from their status of defenders of neo-liberalism as the only game in town. Leaving counter-arguments to be produced and to be effective, this would generate dialogue and consolidate public space, offering a democratic resource for those who would feel necessary to challenge those in power. This is the true power of powerless people, those who successfully challenged the communist dogma in the late decades of socialist regimes in Central and Eastern Europe. With no public sphere, with no decisive arguments arising from the civil society, with no functional voluntary associations which teach the lessons of democracy, civil society and public intellectuals would only form a social body from which those in power would in the end select committed personnel. Submissive intellectuals would legitimate and justify political action of those in power, especially when there is a strong ideological compatibility, as it was the case of public intellectuals in Romania during the populists' rule. Those intellectuals would teach the lessons of conformism, rigidity and would largely help consolidate more and more authoritarian, yet ideologically orthodox political regimes.

The two perspectives briefly exposed here open the way for further research. In the near future, researchers could thoroughly explore the issue of cognitive mobilization and the impact of new communication channels on the participation style among Romanian citizens. Not only in Romania, but in many other countries, new media, social media in general changed the way communication for political purposes is used. In Arab countries, during what is now called the 'Arab Spring', ordinary citizens have succeeded in overcoming the information state control exerted by authoritarian rulers and to get mobilized by the essential means of new communication technologies. This is also true for protesters in Moldova in April 2009, when state-owned radio and television were under tight political control, as it was generally the case with all recent "colored revolutions" in Eastern Europe. Through social media and new facilities, such as SMS sent by cell phones, protesters manage to gather in large numbers in the main town squares in order to put considerable pressure on those in office. The mechanism which turn on-line communication into off-line, street mobilization, lies at the heart of future research.

At the same time, social research could successfully focus on the general framework of democratic consolidation by the functioning of a public sphere, produced by the communication interactions of actors who get engaged in successive and intertwined dialogues. Letting arguments to be decisive and thus defining the common interest, the common reality and the authentic community, this is an essential aspect of democratic consolidation to be unraveled by future research. How arguments are produced and how discursive interactions occur will define democracy in Romania as a space of dialogue, trust and tolerance. The future public role of intellectuals and the common market of ideas are also at the heart of future research. In the end, the two perspectives would continue the current approach set up in this volume, combining the analysis of dominant social values and practices with the focus on elites' behavior. The combined perspective is essential in understanding Romania's democratic trajectory, as well as underlining new challenges which could affect democratic consolidation in Romania.

Bibliography

Abbott, Pamela. 2007. "Cultural Trauma and Social Quality in Post-Soviet Moldova and Belarus." *East European Politics and Societies* 21 (2): 219–258.

Adorno, Theodor. 1980. *The Philosophy of Modern Music*. New York: Seabury.

Agh, Attila. 2014. "Decline of Democracy in East-Central Europe: The Last Decade as the Lost Decade in the ECE Democratization." *Journal of Comparative Politics* 7 (2): 4–33.

Agh, Attila. 2015. "The Bumpy Road of Civil Society in the New Member States: From State Capture to the Renewal of Civil Society." *Politics in Central Europe* 11 (2): 7–21.

Akkerman, Tjitske. 2012. "Comparing Radical Right Parties in Government: Immigration and Integration Policies in Nine Countries." *West European Politics* 35 (3): 511–529.

Albertazzi, Daniele, and Duncan McDonnell (eds.). 2007. *Twenty-First Century Populism: The Spectre of Western European Democracy*. Basingstoke: Palgrave Macmillan.

Albertazzi, Daniele, and Duncan McDonnell. 2010. "The Lega Nord Back in Government." *West European Politics* 33 (6): 1318–1340.

Allina-Pisano, Jessica. 2010. "Social contracts and authoritarian projects in post-Soviet space: the use of administrative resource." *Communist and Post-Communist Studies* 43 (4): 373–382.

Allport, Gordon W. 1961. *Pattern and Growth in Personality*. New York: Holt, Rinehart and Winston.

Almond, Gabriel A., and Sidney Verba. 1963. *The Civic Culture*. Princeton, NJ: Princeton University Press.

Appel, Hilary. 2005. "Anti-Communist Justice and Founding for Post-Communist Order: Lustration and Restitution in Central Europe." *East European Politics and Societies* 19 (3): 379–405.

Arzheimer, Kai. 2015. "The AfD: Finally a Successful Right-Wing Populist Eurosceptic Party for Germany?" *West European Politics* 38 (3): 535–556.

Bădescu, Gabriel. 2003a. "Încredere şi democraţie în ţările în tranziţie." *Sociologie Românească* I (1–2): 109–128.

Bădescu, Gabriel. 2003b. "Social Trust and Democratization in the Post-Communist Societies." In *Social Capital and the Transition to Democracy*, edited by Gabriel Bădescu and Eric Uslaner, 120–139. New York: Routledge.

Bădescu, Gabriel. 2004. "Culture, income tax and social inequality in Romania." *Romanian Journal of Society and Politics* 4 (1): 80–97.

Bădescu, Gabriel, Paul E. Sum, and Eric M. Uslaner. 2004. "Civil Society and Democratic Values in Romania and Moldova." *East European Politics and Societies* 18 (2): 316–341.

Baker, Catherine. 2010. "Popular Music and Political Change in Post-Tudman Croatia: 'It's All the Same, Only He's not Here?'" *Europe-Asia Studies* 62 (10): 1741–1759.

Barnes, Samuel H. 2004a. "Perspectives on Political Action: A Review Twenty-five Years Later." Paper presented at the ECPR Joint Sessions of Workshops, Uppsala, Sweden.

Barnes, Samuel H. 2004b. "Political Participation in Post-Communist Central and Eastern Europe." Center for the Study of Democracy, University of California, Irvine, paper 04-10. Available from: http://repositories.cdlib.org/csd/04-10.

Barnes, Samuel H., and Max Kaase. 1979. *Political Action: Mass Participation in Five Western Democracies.* London: Sage.

Batory, Agnes. 2010. "Kin-state Identity in the European Context: Citizenship, Nationalism, and Constitutionalism in Hungary." *Nations and Nationalism* 16 (1): 31–48.

Berend, Ivan T. 2007. "Social shock in transforming Central and Eastern Europe." *Communist and Post-Communist Studies* 40 (3): 269–280.

Birch, Sarah. 2007. "Electoral Systems and Electoral Misconduct." *Comparative Political Studies* 40 (12): 1533–1556.

Blank, Stephen. 2008. "The Putin Succession and Its Implications for Russian Politics." *Post-Soviet Affairs* 24 (3): 231–262.

Bourdieu, Pierre. 1980. "Le capital social: notes provisoires." *Actes de la Recherche en Sciences Sociales* 31 (1): 2–3.

Bozóki, András. 2016. "Mainstreaming the Far Right: Cultural Politics in Hungary." *Revue d'études comparatives Est-Ouest* 47 (4): 87–116.

Brehm, John, and Wendy Rahn. 1997. "Individual-level evidence for the causes and consequences of social capital." *American Journal of Political Science* 41 (3): 999–1023.

Brubaker, Rogers. 1992. "Citizenship Struggles in Soviet Soviet Successors States." *International Migration Review* 26 (2): 269–291.

Bugaric, Bojan. 2008. "Populism, liberal democracy, and the rule of law in Central and Eastern Europe." *Communist and Post-Communist Studies* 41 (2): 191–203.

Bunce, Valerie J., and Sharon L. Wolchik. 2006. "International diffusion and post-communist electoral revolutions." *Communist and Post-Communist Studies* 39 (3): 283–304.

Căluşer, Monica (ed.). 2009. *Carta europeană a limbilor regionale sau minoritare în România. Între norme şi practici.* Cluj: Ethnocultural Diversity Resource Center Press.

Cameron, David R. 2003. "The Challenges of Accession." *East European Politics and Societies* 17 (1): 24–41.

Careja, Romana. 2011. "Paths to Policy Coherence to Create Market Economies in Central and Eastern Europe." *International Political Science Review* 32 (3): 345–366.

Carey, Henry F. (ed.). 2004. *Romania since 1989: Politics, Economics and Society.* Lanham, MD: Rowman & Littlefield.

Center for the Study of Democracy Bulgaria, Vitosha Research. 2000. *Accountable government: Self and public perception.* http://www.vitosha-research.com/vrartShow.php?id=5470

Chafetz, Glenn R. 1992. "Soviet Ideological Revision and the Collapse of Communism in Eastern Europe." *International Relations* 11 (2): 151–169.

Chen, Cheng. 2003. "The roots of illiberal nationalism in Romania: a historical institutionalist analysis of the Leninist legacy." *East European Politics and Societies* 17 (2): 166–201.

Chiribucă, Dan, and Tivadar Magyari. 2003. "The Impact of Minority Participation in Romanian Government." In *A New Balance: Democracy and Minorities in Post-Communist Europe*, edited by Monica Robotin, and Levente Salat, 73–97. Budapest: Open Society Institute.

Chirot, Daniel (ed.). 1991. *The Origins of Backwardness in Eastern Europe: Economics and Politics from the Middle Ages until the Early Twentieth Century.* Oakland, CA: University of California Press.

Ciobanu, Monica. 2007. "Romania's Travails with Democracy and Accession to the European Union." *Europe-Asia Studies* 59 (8): 1429–1450.

Ciobanu, Monica, 2009. "Criminalising the Past and Reconstructing Collective Memory: The Romanian Truth Commission." *Europe-Asia Studies* 61 (2): 313–336.

Clark, Terry D., and Jill N. Wittrock. 2005. "Presidentialism and the effect of electoral law in postcommunist systems." *Comparative Political Studies* 38 (2): 171–188.

Clarke, Harold, Paul Whiteley, Walter Borges, David Sanders, and Marianne Stewart. 2016. "Modelling the dynamics of support for a right-wing populist party: the case of UKIP." *Journal of Elections, Public Opinion and Parties* 26 (2): 135–154.

Clemens Jr., Walter C. 2010. "Ethnic peace, ethnic conflict: Complexity theory on why the Baltic is not the Balkans." *Communist and Post-Communist Studies* 43 (2): 245–261.

Coleman, James S. 1988. "Social Capital in the Creation of Human Capital." *American Journal of Sociology* 94 (Supplement): 95–119.

Coleman, James S. 1990. *Foundation of Social Theory.* Cambridge, MA: Belknap Press.

Conrad, Courtenay R., and Sona N. Golder. 2010. "Measuring government duration and stability in Central Eastern European democracies." *European Journal of Political Research* 49 (1): 119–150.

Crowther, William. 1998. "Ethnic politics and the post-communist transition in Moldova." *Nationalities Papers* 26 (1): 147–164.

Dahl, Robert A. 1971. *Polyarchy: Participation and Opposition.* New Haven, CT: Yale University Press.

Dalton, Russell J. 1999. "Political Support in Advanced Industrial Democracies." In *Critical Citizens: Global Support for Democratic Governance,* edited by Pippa Norris, 57–77. Oxford: Oxford University Press.

Danero Iglesias, Julien. 2015. "An Ad Hoc Nation: An Analysis of Moldovan Election Campaign Clips." *East European Politics and Societies* 29 (4): 850–870.

Dawisha, Karen. 2005. "Communism as a Lived System of Ideas in Contemporary Russia." *East European Politics and Societies* 19 (3): 463–493.

Dawisha, Karen, and Stephen Deets. 2006. "Political Learning in Post-Communist Elections." *East European Politics and Societies* 20 (4): 691–728.

De Lange, Sarah L., and Simona Guerra. 2009. "The League of Polish Families between East and West, past and present." *Communist and Post-Communist Studies* 42 (4): 527–549.

De Raadt, Jasper. 2009. "Contestable constitutions: Ambiguity, conflict, and change in East Central European dual executive systems." *Communist and Post-Communist Studies* 41 (1): 83–101.

De Waele, Jean-Michel, and Anna Pacześniak (eds.). 2010. *Populism in Europe – defect or symptom of democracy.* Warsaw: Oficyna Naukowa.

Deets, Stephen. 2006. "Reimagining the Boundaries of the Nation: Politics and the Development of Ideas on Minority Rights." *East European Politics and Societies* 20 (3): 419–446.

Deletant, Denis. 2006. *Hitler's Forgotten Ally: Ion Antonescu and His Regime, Romania 1940-1944.* Basingstoke: Palgrave Macmillan.

Dembinska, Magdalena, and Julien Danero Iglesias. 2013. "The Making of an Empty Moldovan Category within a Multiethnic Transnistrian Nation." *East European Politics and Societies* 27 (3): 413–428.

Dimitrova-Grajzl, Valentina, and Eszter Simon. 2010. "Political Trust and Historical Legacy: The Effect of Varieties of Socialism." *East European Politics and Societies* 24 (2): 206–228.

Djilas, Milovan. 1957. *The New Class: An Analysis of the Communist System.* New York: Praeger.

Downs, Anthony. 1957. *An Economic Theory of Democracy.* New York: Addison-Wesley.

Dragoman, Dragoş. 2008. "National identity and Europeanization in post-communist Romania. The meaning of citizenship in Sibiu: European Capital of Culture 2007." *Communist and Post-Communist Studies* 41 (1): 63–78.

Dragoman, Dragoş. 2011a. "Regional inequalities, decentralization and the performance of local governments in post-communist Romania." *Local Government Studies* 37 (6): 647–669.

Dragoman, Dragoş. 2011b. "Activisme civique, protestation et contextes politiques. Comparer la Roumanie et la Suisse." *Sociologie Românească* IX (3): 121–140.

Dragoman, Dragoş. 2012. "Linguistic Pluralism and Citizenship in Romania." In *Language Rights Revisited*, edited by Dagmar Richter, Ingo Richter, Iryna Ulasiuk, and Reeta Toivanen, 267–280. Berlin: Berliner Wissenschafts-Verlag and Oisterwijk: Wolf Legal Publisher.

Dragoman, Dragoş. 2013. "Post-Accession Backsliding: non-ideologic populism and democratic setbacks in Romania." *South-East European Journal of Political Science* 1 (3): 27–46.

Dragoman, Dragoş. 2014. "Transitional justice Romanian style: Condemning the communist ideology, but not the communist oppressors." *Transilvania* 7: 28–35.

Dragoman, Dragoş. 2015a. "Political transformation in Moldova: How citizens evaluate past and future." *Revue d'études comparatives Est-Ouest* 46 (1): 79–109.

Dragoman, Dragoş. 2015b. "Where Have All Marxists Gone? The Intellectual Left, Ideological Debate and Public Space in Post-Communist Romania." *Studia Politica. Romanian Political Science Review* XV (2): 229–248.

Dragoman, Dragoş, and Bogdan Gheorghiţă. 2013. "European conditionality, ethnic control or electoral disarray? The 2011 controversial territorial reform attempt in Romania." *POLIS* 2 (1): 72–93.

Dragoman, Dragoş, and Bogdan Gheorghiţă. 2016. "Regional design, local autonomy and ethnic struggle: Romania's syncopated regionalization." *Europe-Asia Studies* 68 (2): 270–290.

Dragoman, Dragoş, and Camil Ungureanu. 2017. "The Faces of Populism in Post-Communist Romania." In *Populism in Europe: From Symptom to Alternative*, edited by Eckart Woertz, 65–67. Barcelona Center for International Affairs (CIDOB) Report no. 1.

Dragoman, Dragoş, Sabina-Adina Luca, Bogdan Gheorghiţă, and Annamária Kádár. 2012. "Popular music, social capital and the consolidation of public space in post-communist Romania." *Sociologie Românească* X (2): 113–133.

Edwards, Bob, and Michael W. Foley. 1998. "Civil society and social capital beyond Putnam." *American Behavioral Scientist* 42 (1): 124–139.

Ehin, Piret. 2007. "Political support in the Baltic states, 1993-2004." *Journal of Baltic Studies* 38 (1): 1–20.

Eke, Steven M., and Taras Kuzio. 2000. "Sultanism in Eastern Europe: The Socio-Political Roots of Authoritarian Populism in Belarus." *Europe-Asia Studies* 52 (3): 523–547.

Ekiert, Grzegorz, Jan Kubik, and Milada Anna Vachudova. 2007. "Democracy in Post-Communist World: An Unending Quest?" *East European Politics and Societies* 21 (1): 7–30.

Ekman, Joachim. 2009. "Political Participation and Regime Stability: A Framework for Analyzing Hybrid Regimes." *International Political Science Review* 30 (1): 7–31.

Enyedi, Zsolt. 2016. "Populist Polarization and Party System Institutionalization: The Role of Party-Politics in De-democratization." *Problems of Post-Communism* 63 (4): 210–220.

Eriksen, Erik Oddvar. 2005. "An Emerging European Public Sphere." *European Journal of Social Theory* 8 (3): 341–363.

Evans, Geoffrey, and Stephen Whitefield. 1995. "The Politics and Economics of Democratic Commitment: Support for Democracy in Transitional Societies." *British Journal of Political Science* 25 (4): 485–514.

Eyal, Gil, Iván Szelényi, and Eleanor Townsley. 2001. *Making Capitalism without Capitalists: The New Ruling Elites in Eastern Europe.* London: Verso.

Fauvelle-Aymar, Christine, and Michael S. Lewis-Beck. 2008. "TR versus PR: Effects of the French double ballot." *Electoral Studies* 27 (3): 400–406.

Fish, Steven, and Omar Choudhry. 2007. "Democratization and Economic Liberalization in the Postcommunist World." *Comparative Political Studies* 40 (3): 254–282.

Flap, Henk. 1999. "Creation and returns of social capital. A new research program." *La revue Tocqueville/The Tocqueville Review* XX (1): 5–26.

Fowler, Brigid. 2004. "Nation, State, Europe and National Revival in Hungarian Party Politics: The Case of the Millennial Commemorations." *Europe-Asia Studies* 56 (1): 57–83.

Freitag, Markus. 2003. "Social Capital in (Dis)similar Democracies. The Development of Generalized Trust in Japan and Switzerland." *Comparative Political Studies* 36 (8): 936–966.

Frentzel-Zagórska, Janina, and Krzysztof Zagórski. 1989. "East European Intellectuals on the Road of Dissent: The Old Prophecy of a New Class Re-examined." *Politics & Society* 17 (1): 89–113.

Fukuyama, Francis. 1995. *Trust: The Social Virtues and the Creation of Prosperity.* New York: Free Press.

Gallagher, Tom. 2001. "Nationalism and political culture in the 1990s." In *Post-Communist Romania: Coming to Terms with Transition*, edited by Duncan Light, and David Phinnemore, 104–124. Basingstoke: Palgrave Macmillan.

Gallagher, Tom. 2005. *Theft of a Nation: Romania since Communism.* London: Hurst.

Ganev, Georgy. 2005. "Where Has Marxism Gone? Gauging the Impact of Alternative Ideas in Transition Bulgaria." *East European Politics and Societies* 19 (3): 443–462.

Ganev, Venelin. 2013. "Post-Accession Hooliganism: Democratic Governance in Bulgaria and Romania after 2007." *East European Politics and Societies* 27 (1): 26–44.

Gel'man, Vladimir. 2008. "Out of the Frying Pan, into the Fire? Post-Soviet Regime Changes in Comparative Perspective." *International Political Science Review* 29 (2): 157–180.

Gherghina, Sergiu. 2013. "Going for a Safe Vote: Electoral Bribes in Post-Communist Romania." *Debatte: Journal of Contemporary Central and Eastern Europe* 21 (2–3): 143–164.

Gherghina, Sergiu, and Sergiu Miscoiu. 2013. "The Failure of Cohabitation: Explaining the 2007 and 2012 Institutional Crises in Romania." *East European Politics and Societies* 27 (4): 668–684.

Gibson, James L. 2003. "Social Networks, Civil Society, and the Prospects for Consolidating Russia's Democratic Transition." In *Social Capital and the Transition to Democracy*, edited by Gabriel Bădescu and Eric M. Uslaner, 61–80. New York: Routledge.

Giugăl, Aurelian, Ron Johnston, Mihail Chiru, Ionuț Ciobanu, and Alexandru Gavriş. 2017. "Gerrymandering and Malapportionment, Romanian

Style: The 2008 Electoral System." *East European Politics and Societies* 31 (4): 683–703.

Gledhill, John. 2005. "States of Contention: State-Led Political Violence in Post-Socialist Romania." *East European Politics and Societies* 19 (1): 76–104.

Griffin, Christine E. 2011. "The trouble with class: researching youth, class and culture beyond the 'Birmingham School.'" *Journal of Youth Studies* 14 (3): 245–259.

Grigorescu, Alexandru. 2006. "The Corruption Eruption in East-Central Europe: The Increased Salience of Corruption and the Role of Intergovernmental Organizations." *East European Politics and Societies* 20 (3): 516–549.

Grzymala-Busse, Anna. 2007. *Rebuilding Leviathan: Party Competition and State Exploitation in Post-Communist Democracies.* Cambridge: Cambridge University Press.

Habermas, Jürgen. 1989. *The Structural Transformation of the Public Sphere: An Inquiry into a Category of Bourgeois Society.* Cambridge, MA: MIT Press.

Haerpfer, Christian W. 2008. "Support for Democracy and Autocracy in Russia and the Commonwealth of Independent States, 1992-2002." *International Political Science Review* 29 (4): 411–432.

Hale, Henry E. 2006. "Democracy or autocracy on the march? The colored revolutions as normal dynamics of patronal presidentialism." *Communist and Post-Communist Studies* 39 (3): 305–329.

Hartshorne, Charles, and Paul Weiss (eds.). 1934. *Collected Papers of Charles Sanders Peirce. Vol. V. Pragmatism and Pragmaticism.* Cambridge, MA: Harvard University Press.

Hayashi, Nahoko, Elinor Ostrom, John Walker, and Toshio Yamagishi. 1999. "Reciprocity, trust and the sense of control. A cross-societal study." *Rationality and Society* 11 (1): 27–46.

Hein, Michael. 2015. "The Fight Against Government Corruption in Romania: Irreversible Results or Sisyphean Challenge?" *Europe-Asia Studies* 67 (5): 747–776.

Hofferbert, Richard I., and Hans-Dieter Klingemann. 1999. "Remembering the bad old days: human rights, economic conditions, and democratic performance in transitional regimes." *European Journal of Political Research* 36 (2): 155–174.

Hofferbert, Richard I., and Hans-Dieter Klingemann. 2001. "Democracy and Its Discontents in Post-Wall Germany." *International Political Science Review* 22 (4): 363–378.

Holmes, Leslie. 2009. "Crime, organised crime and corruption in post-communist Europe and the CIS." *Communist and Post-Communist Studies* 42 (2): 265–287.

Hooghe, Marc. 2000. "Socialization, Selective Recruitment and Value Congruence. Voluntary associations and the development of shared norms." Paper presented at ECPR Joint Sessions of Workshops, Copenhagen, Denmark.

Hooghe, Marc. 2003. "Participation in Voluntary Associations and Value Indicators: The Effect of Current and Previous Participation Experiences." *Nonprofit and Voluntary Sector Quarterly* 32 (1): 47–69.

Horvath, Robert. 2011. "Putin's 'Preventive Counter-Revolution': Post-Soviet Authoritarianism and the Spectre of Velvet Revolution." *Europe-Asia Studies* 63 (1): 1–25.

Howard, Marc M. 2002a. "The Weakness of Postcommunist Civil Society." *Journal of Democracy* 13 (1): 157–169.

Howard, Marc M. 2002b. *The Weakness of Civil Society in Post-Communist Europe*. New York: Cambridge University Press.

Howard, Marc M. 2003. "Why Post-Communist Citizens Do Not Join Voluntary Organizations." In *Social Capital and the Transition to Democracy*, edited by Gabriel Bădescu and Eric M. Uslaner, 165–183. New York: Routledge.

Huntington, Samuel P. 1968. *Political Order in Changing Societies*. New Haven, CT: Yale University Press.

Huntington, Samuel P. 1991. *The Third Wave: Democratization in the Late Twentieth Century*. Norman, OK: University of Oklahoma Press.

Inglehart, Ronald. 1977. *The Silent Revolution: Changing Values and Political Styles Among Western Publics*. Princeton, NJ: Princeton University Press.

Inglehart, Ronald. 1990. *Culture Shift in Advanced Industrial Society*. Princeton, NJ: Princeton University Press.

Inglehart, Ronald. 1997. *Modernization and Postmodernization: Cultural, Economic and Political Change in 43 Societies*. Princeton, NJ: Princeton University Press.

Institute for Public Policy Moldova. 2009. *Public Opinion Barometer 2009*. http://ipp.md/old/libview.php?l=ro&idc=156&id=454

Iordachi, Constantin. 2001. "The Romanian-Hungarian Reconciliation Process, 1994-2001: From Conflict to Cooperation." *Romanian Journal of Political Science* 1(3–4): 88–133.

Iwasaki, Ichiro, and Taku Suzuki. 2007. "Transition strategy, corporate exploitation, and state capture: An empirical analysis of the former Soviet states." *Communist and Post-Communist Studies* 40 (3): 393–422.

Järve, Priit. 2003. "Language battles in the Baltic States: 1998-2002." In *Ethnicity and Language Politics in Transition Countries*, edited by Farimah Daftary and François Grin, 73–105. Budapest: Open Society Institute.

John, Peter. 2000. "The Europeanisation of Sub-national Governance." *Urban Studies* 37 (5–6): 877–894.

Johnson, Pauline. 2001. "Habermas's Search for the Public Sphere." *European Journal of Social Theory* 4 (2): 215–236.

Jones, Eric. 2007. "Populism in Europe." *SAIS Review of International Affairs* XXVII (1): 37–47.

Killingsworth, Matt. 2010. "Lustration after totalitarianism: Poland's attempt to reconcile with its Communist past." *Communist and Post-Communist Studies* 43 (3): 275–284.

King, Ronald F., and Paul E. Sum (eds.). 2011. *Romania under Basescu: Aspirations, Achievements, and Frustrations during His First Presidential Term*. Lanham, MD: Lexington Books.

Kitschelt, Herbert. 1995. "Formation of Party Cleavages in Post-Communist Democracies: Theoretical Propositions." *Party Politics* 1 (4): 447–472.

Kivinen, Markku, and Terry Cox. 2016. "Russian Modernisation – a New Paradigm." *Europe-Asia Studies* 68 (1): 1–19.

Klingemann, Hans-Dieter. 1999. "Mapping Political Support in the 1990s: A Global Analysis." In *Critical Citizens: Global Support for Democratic Governance*, edited by Pippa Norris, 78–99. Oxford: Oxford University Press.

Kluegel, James R., and David S. Mason. 2004. "Fairness Matters: Social Justice and Political Legitimacy in Post-Communist Europe." *Europe-Asia Studies* 56 (6): 813–834.

Knack, Stephen, and Philip Keefer. 1997. "Does social capital have an economic pay-off? A cross-country investigation." *Quarterly Journal of Economics* 112 (4): 1251–1288.

Konrád, György, and Iván Szelényi, 1979. *The Intellectuals on the Road to Class Power*. New York: Harcourt Brace Jovanovich.

Krastev, Ivan. 2007. "The Strange Death of the Liberal Consensus", *Journal of Democracy* 18 (4): 56–63.

Kriesi, Hanspeter. 2014. "The Populist Challenge." *West European Politics* 37 (2): 381–378.

Kulcsár, László, and Cristina Bradatan. 2007. "Politics without Frontiers: The Impact of Hungarian Domestic Politics on the Minority Question in Romania." *Communist and Post-Communist Studies* 40 (3): 301–314.

Kuzio, Taras. 2001. "Transition in Post-Communist States: Triple or Quadruple." *Politics* 21 (3): 168–177.

Kuzio, Taras. 2005. "Regime type and politics in Ukraine under Kuchma." *Communist and Post Communist Studies* 38 (2): 167–190.

Kymlicka, Will, and François Grin. 2003. "Assessing the Politics of Diversity." In *Ethnicity and Language Politics in Transition Countries*, edited by Farimah Daftary and François Grin, 1–28. Budapest: Open Society Institute.

Lambroschini, Sophie. 2008. "Genèse, apogée et métamorphoses du présidentialisme clientéliste en Ukraine." *Revue d'études comparatives Est-Ouest* 39 (2): 117–148.

Lane, David. 2009. " 'Coloured Revolution' as a Political Phenomenon." *Journal of Communist Studies and Transition Politics* 25 (2–3): 113–135.

Ledyaev, Valeri. 2008. "Domination, Power and Authority in Russia: Basic Characteristics and Forms." *Journal of Communist Studies and Transition Politics* 24 (1): 17–36.

Leipnik, Olena. 2013. "Informal Relations from Democratic Representation to Corruption. Case Studies from Central and Eastern Europe." *Europe-Asia Studies* 65 (1): 152–154.

Leung, Ambrose, and Cheryl Kier. 2008. "Music preferences and civic activism of young people." *Journal of Youth Studies* 11 (4) 445–460.

Levitz, Paul, and Grigore Pop-Eleches. 2010. "Why No Backsliding? The European Union's Impact on Democracy and Governance Before and After Accession." *Comparative Political Studies* 43 (4): 457–485.

Liiceanu, Gabriel. 1992. *Apel către lichele*. Bucharest: Humanitas.

Lijphart, Arend. 1984. *Democracies: Patterns of Majoritarian and Consensus Government in Twenty-One Countries*. New Haven, CT: Yale University Press.

Linz, Juan J. 1990. "The Perils of Presidentialism." *Journal of Democracy* 1 (1): 51–69.

Linz, Juan J., and Alfred Stepan. 1996. *Problems of Democratic Transition and Consolidation: Southern Europe, South America, and Post-Communist Europe*. Baltimore, MD: Johns Hopkins University Press.

Lubecki, Jan, 2004. "Echoes of Latifundism? Electoral Constituencies of Successor Parties in Post-Communist Countries." *East European Politics and Societies* 18 (1): 10–44.

Lühiste, Kari. 2006. "Explaining trust in political institutions: Some illustrations from the Baltic states." *Communist and Post-Communist Studies* 39 (4): 475–496.

Marian, Cosmin G., and Ronald F. King. 2010. "Plus ça change: Electoral law reform and the 2008 Romanian parliamentary elections." *Communist and Post-Communist Studies* 43 (1): 7–18.

Marinova, Dani M. 2011. "When government fails us: trust in post-socialist civil organizations." *Democratization* 18 (1): 160–183.

Matusitz, Jonathan. 2010. "Semiotics of Music: Analysis of Cui Jian's 'Nothing to My Name,' the Anthem for the Chinese Youths in the Post-Cultural Revolution Era." *The Journal of Popular Culture* 43 (1): 156–175.

Mayer, Günter, and Wolfgang Küttner. 2008. "Post-Soviet Marxists in Russia." *Debatte: Journal of Contemporary Central and Eastern Europe* 16 (3): 347–357.

Mazur, Liudmila. 2015. "Golden age mythology and the nostalgia of catastrophes in post-Soviet Russia." *Canadian Slavonic Papers* 57 (3–4): 213–238.

McFaul, Michael. 2002. "The Fourth Wave of Democracy and Dictatorship: Noncooperative Transitions in the Postcommunist World." *World Politics* 54 (2): 212–244.

Mihăilescu, Mihaela. 2008. "The Politics of Minimal "Consensus": Interethnic Opposition Coalitions in Post-Communist Romania (1990-96) and Slovakia (1990-98)." *East European Politics and Societies* 22 (3): 553–594.

Mihuț, Liliana, 1994. "The emergence of political pluralism in Romania." *Communist and Post-Communist Studies* 27 (4): 411–422.

Mink, Georges, and Jean-Charles Szurek. 2002. "Democracy and Capitalism: The Role of the Former Elites in Postcommunist Transformation." *Diogenes* 49 (2): 115–119.

Mishler, William, and Richard Rose. 1996. "Trajectories of Fear and Hope. Support for Democracy in Post-Communist Europe." *Comparative Political Studies* 28 (4): 553–581.

Mishler, William, and Richard Rose. 1997. "Trust, Distrust, and Skepticism: Popular Evaluations of Civil and Political Institutions in Post-Communist Societies." *Journal of Politics* 59 (2): 418–451.

Mishler, William, and Richard Rose. 2001a. "What Are the Origins of Political Trust: Testing Institutional and Cultural Theories in Post-Communist Societies." *Comparative Political Studies* 34 (1): 30–62.

Mishler, William, and Richard Rose. 2001b. "Political Support for Incomplete Democracies: Realist vs. Idealist Theories and Measures." *International Political Science Review* 22 (4): 303–320.

Mishler, William, and Richard Rose. 2005. "What are the Political Consequences of Trust. A Test of Cultural and Institutional Theories in Russia." *Comparative Political Studies* 38 (9): 1050–1078.

Misztal, Barbara. 1996. *Trust in Modern Societies.* Cambridge, MA: Polity Press.

Misztal, Barbara. 2001. "Trust and cooperation: the democratic public sphere." *Journal of Sociology* 37 (4): 371–368.

Møller, Jørgen, and Svend-Erik Skaaning. 2010. "Post-communist regime types: Hierarchies across atributes and space." *Communist and Post-Communist Studies* 43 (1): 51–71.

Moraski, Bryon J. 2013. "Constructing courts after communism: Reevaluating the effect of electoral uncertainty." *Communist and Post-Communist Studies* 46 (4): 433–443.

Mudde, Cas. 2004. "The populist zeitgeist." *Government and Opposition* 32 (3): 541–563.

Mudde, Cas. 2007. *Populist Radical Right Parties in Europe*. Cambridge: Cambridge University Press.

Mudde, Cas. 2010. "The Populist Radical Right: A Pathological Normalcy." *West European Politics* 36 (6): 1167–1186.

Mungiu-Pippidi, Alina, 2003. "Reinventing the Peasants. Local State Capture in Post-Communist Europe." *Romanian Journal of Political Science* 3 (2): 23–38.

Mungiu-Pipiddi, Alina, and Laura Ştefan. 2012. "Perpetual Transition: Contentious Property and Europeanization in South-East Europe." *East European Politics and Societies* 26 (2): 340–361.

Munro, Neil. 2007. "Which Way Does Ukraine Face? Popular Orientations Toward Russia and Western Europe." *Problems of Post-Communism* 54 (6): 43–58.

Mzavanadze, Nora. 2009. "Sustainable development in Lithuania: Between the government agenda and the undiscovered civil society." *Journal of Baltic Studies* 40 (3): 397–414.

Narayan, Deepa, and Michael F. Cassidy. 2001. "A Dimensional Approach to Measuring Social Capital: Development and Validation of a Social Capital Inventory." *Current Sociology* 49 (2): 59–102.

Newton, Kenneth. 1999. "Social Capital and Democracy in Modern Europe." In *Social Capital and European Democracy*, edited by Jan van Deth, 3–24. London: Routledge.

Newton, Kenneth. 2001. "Trust, Social Capital, Civil Society and Democracy." *International Political Science Review* 22 (2): 201–214.

Newton, Kenneth. 2005. "Support for Democracy – Social Capital, Civil Society and Political Performance." WZB Discussion Paper SP IV 2005-402.

Newton, Kenneth, and Pippa Norris. 2000. "Confidence in Public Institutions: Faith, Culture or Performance?" In *Disaffected Democracies: What's Troubling the Trilateral Countries?* edited by

Susan J. Pharr and Robert D. Putnam, 52–73. Princeton, NJ: Princeton University Press.

Norris, Pippa. 1999. "Introduction: The Growth of Critical Citizens." In *Critical Citizens: Global Support for Democratic Governance*, edited by Pippa Norris, 1–30. Oxford: Oxford University Press.

Norris, Pippa. 2000. "Making Democracies Work. Social Capital and Civic Engagement in 47 Societies." Paper for the European Science Foundation EURESCO Conference on Social Capital: Interdisciplinary Perspectives at the University of Exeter, Exeter, UK, 15-20 September.

Norris, Pippa, Stefan Walgrave, and Peter van Aelst. 2005. "Who Demonstrates: Anti-State Rebels, or Conventional Participants? or Everyone?" *Comparative Politics* 37 (2): 251–275.

Noutcheva, Gergana, and Dimitar Bechev. 2008. "The Sucessful Laggards: Bulgaria and Romania's Accession to the EU." *East European Politics and Societies* 22 (1): 114–144.

O'Dwyer, Conor. 2006. "Reforming Regional Governance in East Central Europe: Europeanization or Domestic Politics as Usual?" *East European Politics and Societies* 20 (2): 219–253.

Paldam, Martin, and Gert Tingaart Svendsen. 2001. "Missing social capital and the transition in Eastern Europe." *Journal for Institutional Innovation, Development and Transition* 5: 21–34.

Pappas, Takis S. 2008. "Political Leadership and the Emergence of Radical Mass Movements in Democracy." *Comparative Political Studies* 41 (8): 1117–1140.

Patapievici, Horia-Roman. 1996. *Politice*. Bucharest: Humanitas.

Patapievici, Horia-Roman. 2007. *Despre idei & blocaje*. Bucharest: Humanitas.

Pinior, Jószef. 2007. "Settling Accounts for the Wrongs Done on the Left." *Debatte: Journal of Contemporary Central and Eastern Europe* 15 (2): 271–273.

Pop-Eleches, Grigore. 1999. "Separated at Birth or Separated by Birth? The Communist Successor Parties in Romania and Hungary." *East European Politics and Societies* 13 (1): 117–147.

Pop-Eleches, Grigore. 2001. "Romania's Politics of Dejection", *Journal of Democracy* 12 (3): 156–169.

Pop-Eleches, Grigore. 2007. "Between Historical Legacies and the Promise of Western Integration: Democratic Conditionality after Communism." *East European Politics and Societies* 21 (1): 142–161.

Pop-Eleches, Grigore. 2008, "A party for all seasons: Electoral adaptation of Romanian Communist successor parties." *Communist and Post-Communist Studies* 41 (4): 465–479.

Pop-Eleches, Grigore, and Joshua A. Tucker. 2013. "Associated with the Past? Communist Legacies and Civic Participation in Post-Communist Countries." *East European Politics and Societies* 27 (1): 45–68.

Pop-Eleches, Grigore. 2015. "Pre-Communist and Communist Developmental Legacies." *East European Politics and Societies* 29 (2): 391–408.

Preoteasa, Isabela. 2002. "Intellectuals and the public sphere in post-communist Romania: a discourse analytical perspective." *Discourse & Society* 13 (2): 269–292.

Protsyk, Oleh. 2005a. "Federalism and Democracy in Moldova." *Post-Soviet Affairs* 21 (1): 72–90.

Protsyk, Oleh, 2005b. "Politics of Intraexecutive Conflict in Semipresidential Regimes in Eastern Europe." *East European Politics and Societies* 19 (2): 135–160.

Protsyk, Oleh. 2012. "Secession and hybrid regime politics in Transnistria." *Communist and Post-Communist Studies* 45 (1–2): 175–182.

Przeworski, Adam. 1991. *Democracy and the market: Political and economic reforms in Eastern Europe and Latin America*. Cambridge: Cambridge University Press.

Putnam, Robert D. 1993. *Making Democracy Work: Civic Traditions in Modern Italy*. Princeton, NJ: Princeton University Press.

Putnam, Robert D. 1995a. "Bowling Alone. America's Declining Social Capital." *Journal of Democracy* 6 (1): 65–78.

Putnam, Robert D. 1995b. "Turning in, turning out: The strange disappearance of social capital in America." *PS: Political Science and Politics* 28 (4): 664–683.

Putnam, Robert D. 2000. *Bowling Alone: The Collapse and Revival of American Community*. New York: Simon and Schuster.

Qi, Lingling, and Doh Chull Shin. 2011. "How mass political attitudes *affect* democratization: Exploring the facilitating role critical democrats play in the process." *International Political Science Review* 32 (3): 245–262.

Radin, Dagmar. 2009. "Too Ill to Find the Cure? Corruption, Institutions, and Health Care Sector Performance in the New Democracies of Central and Eastern Europe and Former Soviet Union." *East European Politics and Societies* 23 (1): 105–125.

Rajacic, Agnes. 2007. "Populist Construction of the Past and Future: Emotional Campaigning in Hungary between 2002 and 2006." *East European Politics and Societies* 21 (4): 639–660.

Ram, Melanie H. (2009), "Romania: from laggard to leader?" in *Minority Rights in Central and Eastern Europe*, edited by Bernd Rechel, 180–194. London: Routledge.

Ramet, Sabrina P. 2002. *Balkan Babel: The Disintegration of Yugoslavia from the Death of Tito to the Fall of Milosevic*. Boulder, CO: Westview Press.

Ramet, Sabrina P., Christine M. Hassenstab, and Ola Listhaug (eds.). 2017. *Building Democracy in the Yugoslav Successor States: Accomplishments, Setbacks, and Challenges since 1990*. Cambridge: Cambridge University Press.

Ramet, Sabrina P., and Davorka Matic (eds.). 2007. *Democratic Transition in Croatia: Value Transformation, Education and Media*. College Station, TX: Texas A & M University Press.

Ramet, Sabrina P., Ola Listhaug, and Dragana Dulic (eds.). 2011. *Civic and Uncivic Values: Serbia in the Post-Milosevic Era*. Budapest: Central European University Press.

Roberts, Henry L. 1951. *Rumania: Political Problems of an Agrarian State*. New Haven, CT: Yale University Press.

Rogowski, Ronald. 1974. *Rational Legitimacy: A Theory of Political Support*. Princeton, NJ: Princeton University Press.

Roper, Steven D. 2000. *Romania: The Unfinished Revolution*. New York: Routledge.

Roper, Steven D. 2004. "The Romanian revolution from a theoretical perspective." *Communist and Post-Communist Studies* 27 (4): 401–410.

Roper, Steven D., and Florin Feşnic. 2003. "Historical Legacies and Their Impact on Post-Communist Voting Behavior." *Europe-Asia Studies* 55 (1): 119–131.

Rose-Ackerman, Susan. 2007. "From Elections to Democracy in Central Europe: Public Participation and the Role of Civil Society." *East European Politics and Societies* 21 (1): 31–47.

Rose, Richard. 1998. "Getting Things Done in an Anti-Modern Society: Social Capital Networks in Russia." World Bank, Social Capital Initiative Working Paper. Available from: http://siteresources.worldbank.org/INTSOCIALCAPITAL/Resources/Social-Capital-Initiative-Working-Paper-Series/SCI-WPS-06.pdf. 23 October 2017.

Rose, Richard. 2001. "A Diverging Europe." *Journal of Democracy* 12 (1): 93–106.

Rose, Richard, and Craig Weller. 2003. "What Does Social Capital Add to Democratic Values?" In *Social Capital and the Transition to Democracy*, edited by Gabriel Bădescu and Eric M. Uslaner, 200–218. New York: Routledge.

Rose, Richard, William Mishler, and Christian Haerpfer. 1998. *Democracy and Its Alternatives: Understanding Post-Communist Societies.* Baltimore, MD: Johns Hopkins University Press.

Rothstein, Bo. 2001. "Social Capital in the Social Democratic Welfare State." *Politics & Society* 29 (2): 207–241.

Rothstein, Bo, and Eric M. Uslaner. 2005. "All for All: Equality and Social Trust." Paper to be presented at the European Consortium for Political Research Joint Session of Workshops, Granada, Spain.

Rubenson, Daniel. 2000. "Participation and Politics. Social Capital, Civic Voluntarism, and Institutional Context." Paper presented at European Consortium for Political Research Workshop, Copenhagen.

Rupnik, Jacques. 2007. "From democracy fatigue to populist backlash." *Journal of Democracy* 18 (4): 17–25.

Ryabinska, Natalya. 2011. "The Media Market and Media Ownership in Post-Communist Ukraine: Impact on Media Independence and Pluralism." *Problems of Post-Communism* 58 (6): 3–20.

Sandu, Dumitru. 1999. *Spaţiul social al tranziţiei.* Iaşi: Polirom.

Sandu, Dumitru. 2002. "Diferenţieri europene ale toleranţei sociale." *Sociologie Românească* New Series (1–2): 1–37.

Sartori, Giovanni. 1987. *A Theory of Democracy Revisited.* New York: Chatham House.

Sasse, Gwendolyn. 2004. "Minority Rights and EU Enlargement: Normative Overstretch or Effective Conditionality." In *Minority Protection and the Enlarged European Union,* edited by Gabriel N. Toggenburg, 59–84. Budapest: Open Society Institute.

Schimmelfennig, Frank. 2007. "European Regional Organizations, Political Conditionality, and Democratic Transformation in Eastern Europe." *East European Politics and Societies* 21 (1): 126–141.

Schimmelfennig, Frank, and Ulrich Sedelmeier. 2004. "Governance by Conditionality: EU Rule Transfer to the Candidate Countries of Central and Eastern Europe." *Journal of European Public Policy* 11 (4): 661–679.

Schmitter, Philippe C. 2007. "A Balance Sheet of the Vices and Virtues of 'Populisms.'" *Romanian Journal of Political Science* 7 (2): 5–11.

Seligman, Adam B. 2000. *The Problem of Trust.* Princeton, NJ: Princeton University Press.

Sestanovich, Stephen. 2004. "Force, Money, and Pluralism." *Journal of Democracy* 15 (3): 32–42.

Silitsky, Vitali. 2005. "Preempting Democracy: the Case of Belarus." *Journal of Democracy* 16 (4): 84–97.

Silitsky, Vitali. 2010. " 'Survival of the fittest': Domestic and international dimensions of the authoritarian reaction in the former Soviet Union following the colored revolutions." *Communist and Post-Communist Studies* 43 (3): 339–350.

Sofronov, Vladislav. 2008. "Why I Am a Marxist." *Rethinking Marxism* 20 (3): 356–366.

Spechler, Dina R., and Martin C. Spechler. 2009. "Uzbekistan among the great powers." *Communist and Post-Communist Studies* 42 (3): 353–373.

Stan, Lavinia. 2002. "Moral cleansing Romanian style." *Problems of Post-Communism* 49 (4): 52–62.

Stan, Lavinia. 2004. "Spies, files and lies: explaining the failure of access to Securitate files." *Communist and Post-Communist Studies* 37 (3): 341–359.

Stan, Lavinia. 2006. "The Vanishing Truth: Politics and Memory in Post-Communist Europe." *East-European Quarterly* 40 (4): 383–408.

Stan, Lavinia. 2007. "Goulash Justice for Goulash Communism? Explaining Transitional Justice in Hungary." *Studia Politica. Romanian Political Science Review* VII (2): 269–291.

Stan, Lavinia. 2012. "Which-hunt or Moral Rebirth? Romanian Parliamentary Debates on Lustration." *East European Politics and Societies* 26 (2): 274–295.

Stan, Lavinia, and Lucian Turcescu. 2005. "The Devil's Confessors: Priests, Communists, Spies, and Informers." *East European Politics and Societies* 19 (4): 655–685.

Stark, David and László Bruszt. 1998. *Postsocialist Pathways. Transforming Politics and Property in East Central Europe.* New York: Cambridge University Press.

Ştefan, Laura, and Sorin Ioniţă. 2012. "Romania." In *Nations in Transit 2012,* edited by Freedom House, 431–450. Washington, DC: Freedom House.

Ştefan, Laura, Dan Tapalagă, and Sorin Ioniţă. 2010. "Romania." In *Nations in Transit 2010: Democratization from Central Europe to Eurasia,* edited by Freedom House, 413–431. Washington, DC: Freedom House.

Stiks, Igor. 2010. "The Citizenship Conundrum in Post-Communist Europe: The Instructive Case of Croatia." *Europe-Asia Studies* 62 (10): 1621–1638.

Stockemer, Daniel, and Greg Elder. 2015. "Germans 25 years after reunification – How much do they know about the German Democratic Republic and what is their value judgment of the socialist regime?" *Communist and Post-Communist Studies* 48 (1): 113–122.

Stoica, Cătălin Augustin. 2004. "From Good Communists to Even Better Capitalists? Entrepreneurial Pathways in Post-Socialist Romania." *East European Politics and Societies* 18 (2): 236–277.

Stoica, Cătălin Augustin. 2012. "Fațetele multiple ale nemulțumirii populare: o schiță sociologică a protestelor in Piața Univeristății din ianuarie 2012." *Sociologie Românească* X (1): 3–35.

Stolle, Dietlind. 2000a. "Clubs and Congregations. The Benefits of Joining an Association." ECPR Joint Sessions of Workshops, Copenhagen, Denmark.

Stolle, Dietlind. 2000b. "Social Capital – A New Research Agenda? Toward an Attitudinal Approach." Paper presented at the European Consortium for Political Research Workshop, Copenhagen, Denmark.

Stolle, Dietlind. 2001. "Getting to Trust. An Analysis of the Importance of Institutions, Families, Personal Experiences and Group Membership." In *Politics in Everyday Life: Social Capital and Participation*, edited by Eric M. Uslaner and Paul Dekker, 118–133. London: Routledge.

Stolle, Dietlind, and Thomas R. Rochon. 1998. "Are All Associations Alike? Member Diversity, Associational Type, and the Creation of Social Capital." *American Behavioral Scientist* 42 (1): 47–65.

Stratton, Jon. 1989. "Beyond Art: Postmodernism and the Case of Popular Music." *Theory, Culture and Society* 6 (1): 31–57.

Sum, Paul E. 2005. "Political Mobilization in Romania: Social Capital, Socialization and Political Participation." *Romanian Journal of Society and Politics* 5 (1): 33–55.

Svendsen, Gert Tinggaard. 2003. "Social Capital, Corruption and Economic Growth: Eastern and Western Europe." Department of Economics, Aarhus School of Business working paper 03-21.

Szelényi, Iván, 1987. "The Prospects and Limits of the East European New Class Project: An Auto-critical Reflection on *The Intellectuals on the Road to Class Power*". *Politics & Society* 15 (2): 103–144.

Taggart, Paul. 1995. "New Populist Parties in Western Europe." *West European Politics* 18 (1): 34–51.

Tănăsoiu, Cosmina. 2008. "Intellectuals and Post-Communist Politics in Romania: An Analysis of Public Discourse, 1990-2000." *East European Politics and Societies* 22 (1): 80–113.

Tesser, Lynn M. 2003. "The Geopolitics of Tolerance: Minority Rights Under EU Expansion in East-Central Europe." *East European Politics and Societies* 17 (3): 483–532.

Tismăneanu, Vladimir. 1993. "The Quasi-revolution and its Discontents: Emerging Political Pluralism in Post-Ceaușescu Romania." *East European Politics and Societies* 7 (2): 309–348.

Tsyganov, Andrei P. 2007. "Modern at last? Variety of weak states in the post-Soviet world." *Communist and Post-Communist Studies* 40 (4): 423–439.

Tudoroiu, Theodor. 2011. "Structural factors vs. regime change: Moldova's difficult quest for democracy." *Democratization* 18 (1): 236–264.

Turcescu, Lucian, and Lavinia Stan. 2015. "Church Collaboration and Resistance under Communism Revisited: The Case of Patriarch Justinian Marina (1948-1977)." *Eurostudia* 10 (1): 75–103.

Uhlin, Anders. 2010. "The Structure and Culture of Post-Communist Civil Society in Latvia." *Europe-Asia Studies* 62 (5): 829–852.

Uslaner, Eric M. 2004. "Bowling Alone: Political Participation in a New Democracy." Paper presented at the ECPR Joint Sessions of Workshops, Uppsala, Sweden.

Uslaner, Eric M., 2007a. *Corruption, Inequality, and the Rule of Law.* Cambridge: Cambridge University Press.

Uslaner, Eric M. 2007b. "Tax Evasion, Corruption, and the Social Contract in Transition." Georgia State University, Andrew Young School of Political Studies Working Paper 07-25.

Uslaner, Eric M. 2010. "Segregation, Mistrust and Minorities." *Ethnicities* 10 (4): 415–434.

Uslaner, Eric M. 2013. "Trust and corruption revisited: how and why trust and corruption shape each other." *Quality and Quantity* 47 (6): 3603–3608.

Uslaner, Eric M., and Bo Rothstein. 2016. "The Historical Roots of Corruption: State Building, Economic Inequality and Mass Education." *Comparative Politics* 48 (2): 216–227.

Uslaner, Eric M., and Gabriel Bădescu. 2004. "Honesty, Trust, and Legal Norms in the Transition to Democracy: Why Bo Rothstein Is Better Able to Explain Sweden than Romania." In *Creating Social Trust in Post-Socialist Transition*, edited by János Kornai, Bo Rothstein and Susan Rose-Ackerman, 31–51. New York: Palgrave Macmillan.

Uslaner, Eric M., and Gabriel Bădescu. 2005. "Making the Grade in Transition: Equality, Tranparency, Trust, and Fairness." Paper presented at the European Consortium for Political Research Joint Session of Workshops, Granada, Spain.

Uslaner, Eric M., and Richard S. Conley. 2003. "Civic Engagement and Particularized Trust: The Ties That Bind People to Their Ethnic Communities." *American Political Research* 31 (4): 331–360.

Van Der Meer, Tom. 2001. "In what we trust? A multi-level study into trust in parliament as an evaluation of state characteristics." *International Review of Administrative Sciences* 76 (3): 517–536.

Van Schaik, Ton. 2002. "Social Capital in the European Values Surveys." Paper prepared for the OECD-ONS International Conference on Social Capital Measurement, London.

Varga, Mihai. 2008. "How Political Opportunities Strengthen the Far Right: Understanding the Rise in Far-Right Militancy in Russia." *Europe-Asia Studies* 60 (4): 561–579.

Vasi, Ion Bogdan. 2004. "The Fist of the Working Class: The Social Movements of Jiu Valley Miners in Post-Socialist Romania." *East European Politics and Societies* 18 (1): 132–157.

Verba, Sidney, Key L. Schlozman, and Henry E. Brady. 2000. "Rational Action and Political Activity." *Journal of Theoretical Politics* 12 (3): 243–268.

Verdery, Katherine. 1995. *National Ideology under Socialism. Identity and Cultural Politics in Ceauşescu's Romania.* Berkeley, CA: California University Press.

Völker, Beate, and Henk Flap. 2001. "Weak Ties as a Liability: The Case of East Germany." *Rationality and Society* 13 (4): 397–428.

Wagner, Antonin. 2000. "Reframing 'Social Origins' Theory: The Structural Transformation of the Public Sphere." *Nonprofit and Voluntary Sector Quarterly* 29 (4): 541–553.

Wallace, Claire, and Rossalina Latcheva. 2006. "Economic Transformation Outside the Law: Corruption, Trust in Public Institutions and the Informal Economy in Transition Countries of Central and Eastern Europe." *Europe-Asia Studies* 58 (1): 81–102.

Warren, Mark E. 1999. "Civil Society and Good Governance." Paper published as part of the U.S. Civil Society Project, Georgetown Public Policy Institute, Georgetown University.

Waterbury, Mark A. 2006. "Internal Exclusion, External Inclusion: Diaspora Politics and Party-Building Strategies in Post-Communist Hungary." *East European Politics and Societies* 20 (3): 483–515.

Way, Lucan A. 2003. "Weak States and Pluralism: The Case of Moldova." *East European Politics and Societies* 17 (3): 454–482.

Way, Lucan A., and Steven Levitsky. 2007. "Linkage, Leverage, and the Post-Communist Divide." *East European Politics and Societies* 21 (1): 48–66.

Welzel, Christian. 2007. "Are Levels of Democracy Affected by Mass Attitudes? Testing Attainment and Sustainment Effects on Democracy." *International Political Science Review* 28 (4): 397–424.

Whiteley, Paul. 1999. "The Origins of Social Capital." In *Social Capital and European Democracy*, edited by Jan van Deth, Marco Maraffi, Kennetk Newton and Paul Whiteley, 23–41. New York: Routledge.

Williams, Colin C., and John Round. 2008. "The Illusion of Capitalism in Post-Soviet Ukraine." *Debatte: Journal of Contemporary Central and Eastern Europe* 16 (3): 331–345.

Wollebaek, Dag, and Per Selle. 2002. "Does Participation in Voluntary Associations Contribute to Social Capital? The Impact of Intensity, Scope, and Type." *Nonprofit and Voluntary Sector Quarterly* 31 (1): 32–61.

World Values Survey. 2005. *World Values Survey Wave 5, 2005–2009.* http://www.worldvaluessurvey.org/WVSOnline.jsp

Yamagishi, Toshio and Midori Yamagishi. 1994. "Trust and Commitment in United States and Japan." *Motivation and Emotion* 18 (2): 129–166.

Zamfira, Andreea, and Dragoş Dragoman. 2009. "Le vote (non)ethnique en Roumanie, 2000-2008. Les performances électorales des partis des minorités allemande et hongroise en perspective comparée." *Revue d'Etudes Comparatives Est-Ouest* 40 (2): 127–156.

Zielonka, Jan. 2007. "The Quality of Democracy after Joining the European Union." *East European Politics and Societies* 21 (1): 162–180.

Zmerli, Sonja, and Ken Newton. 2008. "Social trust and attitudes towards democracy." *Public Opinion Quarterly* 72 (4): 706–724.